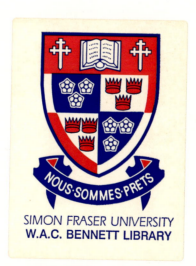

International Perspectives on Tele-Education and Virtual Learning Environments

Edited by
GRAHAM ORANGE and **DAVE HOBBS**
Leeds Metropolitan University

Ashgate

Aldershot • Burlington USA • Singapore • Sydney

Published by
Ashgate Publishing Limited
Gower House
Croft Road
Aldershot
Hampshire GU11 3HR
England

Ashgate Publishing Company
131 Main Street
Burlington
Vermont 05401
USA

Ashgate website: http://www.ashgate.com

British Library Cataloguing in Publication Data
International perspectives on tele-education and virtual
    learning environments
    1. Educational technology - Social aspects 2.Distance
    learning 3.Interactive multimedia - Social aspects
    4. Computer-assisted instruction - Social aspects
    I.Orange, Graham II. Hobbs, Dave
    371.3'58

Library of Congress Catalog Card Number: 99-75450

ISBN 0 7546 1202 3

Printed and bound by Athenaeum Press, Ltd.,
Gateshead, Tyne & Wear.

Contents

List of Figures and Tables

Foreword

HARRIET MAYOR FULBRIGHT
AUSTRALIAN EMBASSY, PARIS, FRANCE

I am delighted to be asked to provide a foreword to this book of *International Perspectives on Tele-Education and Virtual Learning Environments*. The contributors to the book cover a variety of important topics, all designed to stimulate discussion about issues of critical importance to the academic community.

My own interests are particularly focussed on culture and politics, which are often thought of in the United States as warring factions, areas of endeavour which make not just strange but hostile bedfellows. Fortunately the majority of the world's nations view the obvious link between them with greater equanimity, and so in this setting I would like to take a broad look at both fields. There are, as I have mentioned before, startling differences between the history of human invention and the history of human relations. While it seems as if we have made little headway in settling our political differences without resorting to murder and mayhem, invention in this last century has made remarkable progress. One need only note the Wright Brothers' flight of 120 feet and compare it to the moon landing less than 70 years later. Or recall the first national radio broadcast made in the year of my husband's birth and then bring to mind countless recent television news bulletins, flashed on screens in full colour moments after an event has taken place.

Many attribute the growth of governments by and for the people to this explosive development of mass communication. Because of the ability to work in concert with others while at home and to form ever wider networks through electronic media, citizens the world over are able to demand and establish political institutions which are more mindful of popular needs and opinions. The coup against Gorbachev is said to have failed thanks to the fax machine and television coverage. The Berlin Wall and all that it represented fell sooner and more swiftly than was expected in large measure because people could communicate and coordinate with one another. Russia, after over 70 years under a dictatorial one-party system, is now governed by representatives elected by its people, and Germany is now one democratic nation. And Jody Williams, through the use of her computer and fax machine in rural Vermont, created a worldwide organization powerful enough to persuade 80 countries around the world to ban the production and dissemination of land mines.

But the very inventions that seem to strengthen democratic institutions also allow for disturbing developments. Cultures all over the world, no matter how different, are all bent on improving their standards of living without regard to unintended but powerful side effects. This automatically results in altering not only their own immediate surroundings but in influencing - and usually damaging - the basic functioning of the planet as a whole. Environmentalist Bill McKibben has described with eloquence the changes our behaviour imposes on those places we do not inhabit – changes in the way the weather works, changes in the plants and animals that live at the poles or deep in the jungle. This is total. If you need further convincing, the UN's Intergovernmental Panel on Climate Change projects that an immediate 6% reduction in fossil-fuel use is necessary just to stabilize climate at the current level of disruption.

It will take dramatic changes in the cultures of every developed country around the globe, spearheaded by clear-headed well informed thoughtful political leaders working with scientists, businessmen, artists and those in every facet of the humanities, all working together. There is a great deal of pessimism about the feasibility of any behaviour modification, but some startling changes in response to conditions are happening without conscious political intervention. According to Bill McKibben:

"New demographic evidence shows that it is at least possible that a child born today will live long enough to see the peak of human population. Around the world people are choosing to have fewer children - not just in China, where the government forces it on them, but in almost every nation outside the poorest parts of Africa. Population growth rates are lower than they have been at any time since the Second World War. In the past three decades, the average woman in the developing world, excluding China, has gone from bearing six children to bearing four....If this keeps up, the population of the world will not quite double again; United Nations analysts offer as their mid-range projection that it will top out at 10 to 11 billion, up from just under six billion at the moment. The world is still growing, at record pace - we add a New York City every month, almost a Mexico every year, almost an India every decade. But the rate of growth is slowing... [and] if current trends hold, the world's population will all but stop growing before the twenty-first century is out."

In other words, we can and do alter our ways when we see an immediate and pressing need. Large numbers of children in the developed industrial world no longer provide the hands needed to work the land. They are instead a costly addition to a household, and so large families are shrinking. Other patterns of behaviour, however, do not produce results as clearly and immediately detrimental to daily life, thus making new approaches less palatable, more difficult to bring about. Problems such as fossil fuel emissions are not Gordian knots, but they feel more distant, and their solution requires sacrifice. In other words, technology has given great power to each and every one of us, should we perceive a pressing problem or an injustice, but we still seem far away from using that power to tackle the life threatening problems facing all of us on this planet.

What is required is a different state of mind. The problems before us can be solved mechanically, through the use of technology and a reallocation of priorities and resources, but we are hampered by our attitudes. The problems currently confronting us seem to be principally problems of our culture - problems mired in ways of living and thinking built up and transmitted from one generation to another. And this is not a new revelation. Fifteen years ago Jonas Salk wrote of our lack of wisdom when facing the kind of issues that require hard choices.

What are the bases for these problems of the mind, this apparent lack of wisdom? One source of these problems appears to be an insufficient expression of certain qualities which we possess: insufficient generosity, insufficient respect for the rights and the lives of others, insufficient concern for nature and the environment, insufficient development of a perspective which includes all of humankind as opposed to merely one's own self, one's family, one's community, or one's nation. Another source of these problems appears to be an over-sufficient expression of certain other desires, attributes and characteristics which we possess: desire to preserve and expand one's own sphere of life (self, family, community, nation) independent of the effect on others, desire to obtain more wealth and power, the orientation to compete to acquire the most for oneself at the expense of others, the orientation that in the game of life some will be winners and others losers.

This orientation still persists, despite the massive amount of information flooding the world every minute of every day, despite the impressive amount of knowledge we have gained about psychology - new and successful methods of understanding and relating to one another. People are struggling with a monumental amount of misunderstanding and hostility, even among groups that have lived next to each other for years. Witness the former Yugoslavia, where brutal killing and slow torture have been commonplace among neighbours.

What is required is a different approach. Let me give you a few examples of a different mindset - a person or group looking for a long-term solution rather than a means to punish or put down.

During the Second World War, one American prison camp was sent a new commander who called all the German prisoners to order the first morning and demanded all college graduates to step out front. As soon as they gathered, he organized them into an ad hoc faculty, requisitioned books and writing materials, and ordered them to begin teaching the rest. They had to perform a certain amount of hard labour, but the better part of each day was devoted to education. The normal prison camp problems - fights and escape attempts - virtually disappeared, and after the war, the United States found itself with a prison camp full of lifelong friends.

Our prisons are no different. When prisoners are educated, recidivism plummets. Harsh punitive methods breed harsh reactions and more crime, but the prevailing attitude today is that people who break the law should not be coddled or given anything of benefit while locked up. It is a vengeful attitude that focuses on retribution rather than results.

What is needed now is a concerted effort to deal with the fundamental changes in conditions around us – a laser-like focus on feasible means to affect the necessary changes. Among those holding the most promise is the development of learning opportunities that apply and extend knowledge for all citizens; learning opportunities of world-class quality; opportunities accessible to learners worldwide (as individuals or in groups) for their own social and professional fulfilment; learning opportunities that are adaptable to changing technological, social and economic conditions; learning opportunities that are genuine, varied, relevant and meaningful and engage our thoughts, emotions, imagination, predispositions and physiology.

Our understanding of human learning has moved away from the conviction that knowledge is a discreet, objective substance that can be deposited directly in people's minds while they sit in classrooms and lecture halls. As the Institute for Research in Learning has shown, learning is inseparable from engagement in the world, and intellect is inseparable from human experience. This is one of the most important reasons why the international educational exchange that bears my husband's name was and is so successful. And we now have new media, new tools and new motivations to broaden the scope and frequency of these engagements, not as a replacement but an enhancement and an addition to the overseas experience.

Information technology, globalised markets, transportation, and trade agreements have accelerated the movement of learning opportunities to all parts of the globe, to learners of all cultures and nationalities. Transnational education is the remote delivery across national borders of courses, programs and offerings in place-based, telecommunicated and virtual environments creating new communities of learners and new ways of discovering, unhindered by man-made structures and unfettered by regulatory barriers. The power of transnational education is perhaps best illustrated with cases.

Consider the first year higher education student forced to return home from a developed nation because of currency conversion problems. Rather than suspending her study, she discovers an off-campus program distance education offering where content is delivered via a combination of audio, video and computer technologies. It is not recognized by her own Ministry of Education but her institution will accept up to 60 hours of the credit. Despite the temporary financial exigencies facing her and her family, she is able to continue her study, transfer academic credit back into her degree program and graduate on time.

Consider also some national cases. I met recently with the Ambassador to the United States from Malta. Small countries such as Malta are looking to alternative modes of education such as that delivered electronically to augment their small higher education systems that are usually a single national university. In other countries such as Malaysia, China, Singapore, South Africa and the countries of Eastern and Central Europe, the student demand outnumbers the availability of educational offerings. These countries are looking outside of their borders for the education of their national citizens.

If there is one more thing certain beyond death and taxes, it is that the demand for higher education promises will continue to grow. IDP Education Australia estimates that by the year 2025 there will be 159 million students at universities throughout the world. We can no longer be constrained by physical plant, and alternatives are already emerging. In the United States alone, 1994-95 records show there were an estimated 753,640 students formally enrolled in 25,730 distance education courses.

Policy makers from the regulating community, higher education, business and government worldwide are today giving careful thought to transnational education. Its fundamental purpose is principled advocacy, to connect learners globally to quality-assured transnational educational opportunity, so that they, in turn, will use knowledge garnered from the experiences and new learning communities to participate more fully within their respective societies.

Looking to our national policy makers, my husband used to say that we have the representation we deserve, that only through a thoughtful, committed and responsible citizenry will democracy flourish. The present percentages of people who show up at the polls on Election Day are a sad commentary on popular willingness to make our democracy work, and putting the blame on a good economy for this indifference does not acknowledge its deeper significance. Parents and schools, local and national leaders should all shoulder the blame for not putting a high priority on teaching the importance of political participation, for not becoming models in its practice. Senator Fulbright spoke from an international perspective, but his view applies to small groups of people as well as to the planet:

> "Our future is not in the stars but in our own minds and hearts. Creative leadership and liberal education, which in fact go together, are the first requirements for a hopeful future for humankind. Fostering these – leadership, learning, and empathy between cultures – was and remains the purpose of the international scholarship program that I was privileged to sponsor in the U.S. Senate over forty years ago. It is a modest program with an immodest aim – the achievement in international affairs of a regime more civilized, rational and humane than the empty system of power of the past. I believed in that possibility when I began. I still do."

The Editors

Graham Orange is a Principal Lecturer at Leeds Metropolitan University. Prior to joining the University Graham spent many years as a systems developer, business systems analyst and systems consultant, specialising in information systems development methodologies and information strategy planning. Since joining the University Graham has continued offering systems consultancy and has supported this with research into cultural and behavioural issues of information systems development.

Dr Dave Hobbs is a Senior Lecturer at Leeds Metropolitan University where he heads the Virtual Learning Environments Research Group. Six PhD students and five members of staff are currently working on research projects in this area that centre on the development of virtual computer-generated environments whose aim is to stimulate and assist students' learning. This involves designing appropriate visual representation of learners and learning artefacts as well as mechanisms to support the psychological and sociological aspects of distance learning and computer assisted collaborative working. Dave has presented this work at a number of international conferences and published the findings in conference proceedings and journal articles.

1 A Virtual Laboratory for Remote Electronic Engineering Education

ANDREA BAGNASCO, MARCO CHIRICO, GIANCARLO PARODI,
ANDREA SAPPIA AND ANNA MARINA SCAPOLLA
UNIVERSITY OF GENOA, ITALY

Abstract

New open education and training systems can offer a possible solution to the increasing demand for new models of learning. In this chapter, an interactive learning environment for practice in electronic measurement methodologies is presented, providing remote access to real and simulated laboratories. The software model used to implement the environment can be also applied to industrial equipment for remote monitoring end control of devices and remote training of personnel.

Introduction

New learning trends

The exponential development and diffusion of information technologies over the last few years have produced a great acceleration toward the "information society".

The relevance of the subject at international level is confirmed in the "EU Framework V Program", addressed to the information society applications for education and training (DG V report, 1997), and whose main objectives are:

- the enhancement of effectiveness of learning process;
- the increase in development of multimedia educational material aimed at high-quality training programmes;

1

- the improvement of methods and techniques for the "open" distribution of training material and the interoperability of resources of the system.

In the last few years Computer-Based Learning (CBL) technologies have been the object of a considerable amount of research and development activity. The increase in the number of students in higher education colleges and universities and the growing demand for professional, continuous and corporate training have posed serious problems that may be solved with the use of new information technologies and methodologies. These methodologies may play an important role in various systems of education and improve the effectiveness of research and education.

More recently the research activities in CBL have taken advantage of computer networks capabilities, a driving force in new technologies for education that is addressing client-server dynamics and network services. The growth of communication resources such as the Internet have changed the traditional way of supporting learning and training activities as well as production and distribution of learning materials and publications (Bergeron et al., 1996) leading to new Distance Learning (DL) scenarios. The impact of information technology on teaching methods has been driven mainly by:

- the improvements in multimedia technology,
- the success of the World Wide Web (WWW) as global-network accessible information 9berners-Lee, 1996).

The main advantages of WWW based courseware are:

- location and time independent delivery of course material with a large number of possible concurrent attendees;
- simple and familiar interfaces (browser-centric approach);
- reduced time spent from the pedagogical material creation or upgrading to real use;
- different strategies of learning addressed to differentiate students curricula by means of customisable guided tours through course material (McCormack et al. Ponta et al. 1996, Sun et al. 1996, Kahn).

The increasing complexity of such Web based educational environments has led to the development of dedicated frameworks addressed to their creation and maintenance. Nowadays useful tools are available to help the author of courseware to build and manage an educational Web site with full multimedia data synchronisation capabilities and communication facilities between teachers and students (Webct, Ariadne, Imlearn, LearnLinc).

On the learner side, there is a trend towards a larger autonomy of the trainee who chooses personalised training curricula and towards the progressive overcoming of the limitations of times and places that characterise conventional educational systems. This process leads to a new educational paradigm, based on virtual classes. A teacher makes available didactical material on the network and follows and guides the learners using electronic communication tools. The virtual approach is suitable for continuous education, distance learning, and professional training, and broadens to encompass the citizen (not only the specialist) in his/her whole life Cresson, 1996).

It is worth noting that practice is an important component in most of the technical disciplines and so far, this issue seems not to have been addressed by actual distance education environments. Didactical material simulating real experience can improve the knowledge of technical topics but it is well known that simulations are expensive in terms of software development and runtime resources. The basic idea of "learning by doing" suggests a new approach oriented to provide access to virtual laboratories where instruments are available and experiences can be easily set up. In this chapter we present the model of a virtual laboratory, accessible through the Internet, and its application to analogue and digital electronics education.

Learners' needs

The specific approach described in this chapter tries to address the needs of the following potential users:

- university students for practice both in the real laboratories and in a distant learning context;
- industrial trainees;
- industrial and academic researchers willing to share expensive equipment like Automatic Test Equipments (ATE), Computer Aided Design (CAD) tools and libraries.

The number of users involved can vary a lot according to the different user groups; however some basic IT knowledge is required. In the case of University students the number of users is medium-high. Universities and high educational institutions often have to face the problem of overcrowded experimental laboratories due to their limited budget and the lack of technical personnel. This leads to limited access to the laboratories, the impossibility of repeating the experiences, lack of direct assistance and the unavailability of the most expensive and up-to-date instrumentation. Nowadays most of the training laboratories equipped with instrumentation are accessible only at a local site, and each test station can be used by one single user at a time. Such an arrangement has several disadvantages; in particular, the need for the presence of qualified laboratory assistants while experiments are carried out by the students has the consequence that valuable instrumentation is used only for a limited amount of hours during the day.

Another waste comes from the fact that most of the time spent by the students is dedicated to the analysis of test results, while the instrumentation is in a stand-by mode. The availability of the remote control of a set of test stations would allow the users to share instrumentation in a more efficient manner, since the time spent for result analysis is carried out by interacting with a low-cost computer, while the measurement is remotely carried out in a virtually simultaneous way by more groups of students controlling the same equipment. The efficiency of the measurement system is greatly improved in this way. Moreover, the instrumentation can be arranged in a suitably chosen environment so that a limited supervision of laboratory assistants is required, while the students can carry out the experiments from far-apart located sites equipped only with computers, including from their home.

On the other hand, students following 'distance learning' courses often suffer from a too theoretical approach to subjects; for specific disciplines, as in the case of electronic engineering, the capability of carrying out 'experiments' is of outmost importance for the full understanding of the various subjects. Until now, the use of telematics for education and training has been limited to the development of remote course delivery and distance teaching, library services and on-line catalogues, telepresence and distribution of learning materials. Most of these tools are based on computer simulations. The specific problem of providing laboratory courses has been neglected. In these days, certified industries are enforced by EC standards to solve measurement problems by using computer-controlled instrumentation. For this reason, an increased need exists for training highly qualified technical personnel to the use of computer-controlled instrumentation and test stations. The development of distance learning tools would be of help for industry, which, (especially in the case of small and medium enterprises) possibly cannot afford the cost of duplicating their laboratories for training purposes.

In summary, the proposed approach provides the following advantages:

- students (users) can remotely operate laboratories, thus enlarging the opportunities of training for individuals/students living in isolated areas, and for disabled people;

- laboratory instruments can be used by more than one person at a time, thereby reducing the danger of overcrowding and of lack of specialised personnel;

- students can 'design' their own experiment and they can repeat other researchers' experiments if they wish;

- high-cost instruments can be shared by a lot of researchers avoiding incomplete use of resources;

- better opportunities are offered for exchanging scientific results and ideas among researchers and enhancing the co-operation between the academic and the industrial community;

- emulated laboratories can become part of distance learning curricula, with all the related advantages;

- standardisation of course/laboratories format can ease authoring, enlarging the availability of teaching/training material;

- specific products for creating remotely accessible/emulated laboratories can be developed.

The Virtual Laboratory

The concept

The term 'virtual laboratory' refers to a representation of the laboratory that is distributed on the network and allows access to and control of the real laboratory instrumentation and experiences via their software simulation.

The Virtual Instrumentation concept was pioneered in the mid eighties and soon became a revolution in the way the instrumentation was conceived and used. As products and systems grew in complexity, testing and test equipment became more expensive and, at the same time, a critical focus for many companies. Today, manufacturing companies face three major challenges in testing:

- increasing testing costs

- proliferation of test systems;

- cost of the investment in testing throughout the product life cycle.

Virtual instrumentation helps to meet these problems in a timely and cost-effective manner. Moreover virtual instrumentation systems dramatically reduce the time required to develop complex test programs and show a way of working for the unification of the separate worlds of test and measurement (T&M) and industrial automation. With today's software tools, code reuse is an inherent part of the process.

In this project we apply the concept of virtual laboratory to the technical discipline of electronic measurement and testing. The students interact with electronic instrumentation like complex electronic devices, automatic test equipment, industrial control systems, and instruments controlled through IEEE488 or a VXI bus. The didactical target is to practise using instruments and to conduct experiments addressing the knowledge of measurement methods.

Commercially available remote measurement system, such as National Instruments (National Instruments) and Hewlett-Packard VEE Hewlett Packard have interesting features for the development of distance learning tools for electronic laboratory courses. However, in their current form they only partially meet our purposes, since they have not been designed for an educational context in a remote multi-user environment. To our knowledge, at the moment there are no distance learning tools adopting similar tools; the lack of standardization in the field also limits potential applications.

The architecture

In the scheme that we are going to describe, the student always interacts with the virtual laboratory according to a client-server methodology via a Web browser. The virtual laboratory system is organised in three layers from top to bottom: the client layer, the virtual laboratory layer, the (simulated or real) laboratory layer (Figure 1).

The client layer lets the student remotely access the virtual laboratory and being implemented by a common Web browser, opens the system to the Internet community. The virtual laboratory layer offers different functionality such as:

- a presentation of the virtual laboratory and its aims,
- a way to access and control of the laboratory instrumentation and experiences through a user interface,
- the capability of driving instruments,
- multi-user access control,
- communication services and co-operative work tools to support
- the remote measurement and testing activity.

Figure 1 depicts the VL and shows the access to both a real lab and a simulated lab. The real laboratory can consist of one instrument or of a collection of instruments managed by a server via commercial buses like IEEE488 or VXI. The simulated laboratory is instead a collection of software libraries that emulate the behaviour of the real instruments, reacting to the operator commands and generating correct data depending on the experiment. The possibility of operating both simulated and real world using the same interface is one of the main aims of the implementation. This represents an effective way of satisfying the different users' needs previously analysed.

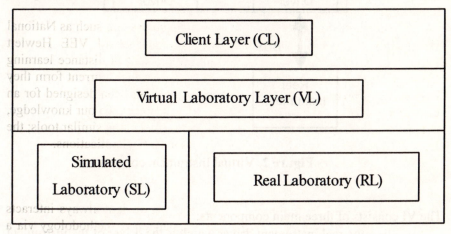

Figure 1 Virtual Laboratory layers

The implementation

The VL can deal with a generic device under electronic control or testing such as a single electronic instrument, a collection of electronic instruments, or an integrated electronic measurement bench. The Virtual Instrument (VI) is the building block of the VL. In Figure 2, the virtual instrument components are shown. The main scope of the VI is to drive a real instrument or its simulated implementation.

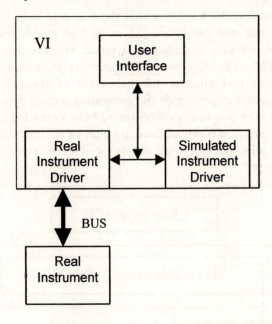

Figure 2 Virtual Instrument components

The VI consists of three main components:
- the real instrument driver which is the driver of the instrument that lets the user directly control the real instrument via command strings;
- the simulated instrument driver which emulates the behaviour of the real instrument;
- the user interface that lets the user interact with the instrument performing the same actions of the real control panel. It is implemented using web-oriented technologies.

Both in the real and in the simulated case, the interaction between the user and the instrument is implemented through the user interface that generates a unique stream of data to be sent to the drivers. The components of the VI can be distributed on different platforms, exchanging information on the network (Figure 3).

The user interface is distributed by a web server to the client browsers, while different implementations have been studied for the interaction between the user interface and the instrument driver. This

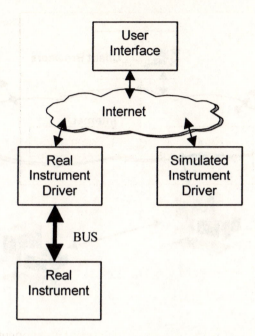

Figure 3 Virtual Instrument architecture

approach takes advantage of the Internet in order to realise a virtual distributed and open environment for training and testing.

The VL can be constituted by a single VI or a collection of VIs interacting to conduct an experiment. In the first case the user interface distributed corresponds to the control panel of the instrument; in the other case the user interface contains the control panels of the VIs and the device under test. We have studied two different implementations for the distribution of the VL.

One implementation is based on a web server that distributes HTML documents describing the VL scope and managing the interaction between the user and the VL by means of Common Gateway Interface (CGI) programs. In Figure 4, this solution is shown. The user can read on the browser the actual status of the control panels of the instrumentation and send command strings to the instruments compiling forms and selecting sensitive maps on the HTML page. The CGI programs implement the interaction with the instruments translating this information into commands and retrieving the results of the operations. The results are then translated into HTML pages and sent back to the clients.

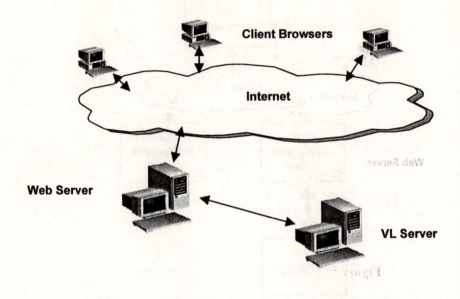

Figure 4 Virtual Laboratory implementation scheme

In Figure 5 the second implementation scheme is presented. The web server contains HTML documents that describe the VL functionality. The web server distributes the VL user interface, to be executed on the client platform. The VL interface contains the VI user interfaces that interact via TCP/IP with the drivers. In the previous approach all the communications were based on the HTTP protocol and managed by the web server; in this case a direct communication channel is set up and the web server only introduces to the VL.

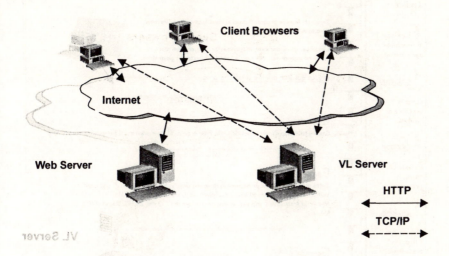

Figure 5 Virtual Laboratory implementation scheme 2

An Electronic Instrumentation Laboratory for Measurement

The VL model has been applied to the education on electronics during engineering graduation curricula. In the prototype, the VL components have been developed using the Labview software from National Instruments. The purpose of this application is to integrate the training with practical experimentation in order to acquire knowledge about measurement methodologies on electronic circuits and, at the same time, gain the capability to operate laboratory instrumentation. The students are introduced to the VL by hypertext pages (see Figure 6) that describe the environment and guide them through the execution of the experiments that can be both totally simulated and carried out on real instrumentation.

The VL consists of a set of electronic instruments (eg oscilloscope, multimeter, and function generator) and a set of circuits under test (eg resistor networks, low-bandwidth filters). In the real case, the instruments are connected to a PC server via an IEEE488 bus.

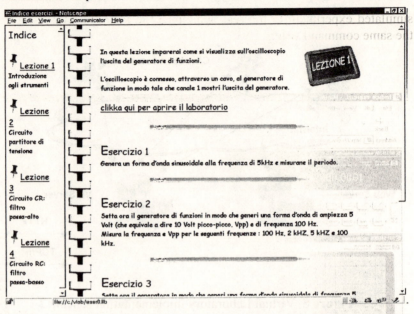

Figure 6 Example VL hypertext page

In the simulated case, the laboratory is based on two software libraries: the instrument library and the circuit library. The user interface of the VL presents the list of the available exercises/lectures. According to the user's choice, the system provides the instruments panels and a menu for the experiment set-up. The student can set the circuit components parameters, where required, and start operating the instruments. In Figure 7 an exercise involving an oscilloscope, a function generator and a circuit under test is shown. The student has to set the capacitor and resistor values and the system then calculates the cut-off frequency of the circuit. Then he/she switches on the instruments and studies the circuit response varying the waveform characteristics and tuning the oscilloscope to visualise the output signal.

The experiment presented in Figure 7 is a simulation; in the case of a real experiment the instruments interfaces do not change but the circuit under test cannot be directly modified. It is possible to set up different circuit boards and let the student to switch among them in a guided way. In the case of real complex and expensive instrumentation, the experimental set-up will be carried on in co-operation with laboratory personnel. Only minor changes are required to adapt the user interface to move from the simulated experiment to the real one, since the instruments drivers accept the same command strings.

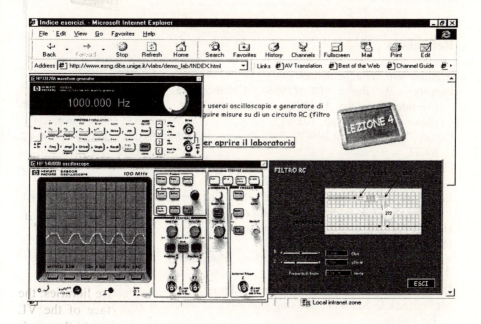

Figure 7 Experiment simulation

Conclusions and Future Work

A virtual approach to access laboratories via network has been presented. The main benefits are the flexibility of the model that can address in a transparent way both real and simulated instrumentation and the reduced cost of the clients needed to access the environment. Possible utilisation is in the field of distance education and training and for the remote control of industrial processes. Future work will be concerned with the development of further applications based on this technique in order to study possible extensions of the model. Didactic experiments will be carried on during the courses of electronics to verify the effectiveness of the environment and its pedagogical results.

In the field of factory automation, the same techniques can be applied to PC controlled environments and monitoring systems.

Acknowledgements

This research has been carried out in co-operation with Ing. Andrea Cambiaso of Quanta Srl.

References

Ariadne. http://ariadne.unil.ch

Bergeron B. Bailin M. (1996); Collaborative Hypermedia Development: Considerations for Academic Publishing, *Jl. of Educational Multimedia and Hypermedia*, 5 (2), pp. 101-112.

Berners-Lee T. (1996); WWW: Past, Present, and Future, *IEEE Computer*, Oct., pp. 69-77.

Cresson E. Flynn P. (1996); Teaching and learning, towards the learning society, *UE White Paper*, DG XII e DG V, Bruxelles.

European Community DG V (1997); Building the European Information Society for us all, *Final report of the High Level Group of Experts*.

Hewlett Packard, http://www.tmo.hp.com/

Imlearn, http://www.imlearn.com/.

Khan B.H.; Web-Based Instruction, *Educational Technology Publications* Englewood Cliffs.

LearnLinc, http://www.ilinc.com/learnl~1.htm.

McCormack C. Jones D., *Building a web-based education system*, Wiley Computer Publishing.

National Instruments, http://www.natins.com.

Ponta D. Scapolla A.M. Taini M. (1996); Telematics for education: The design of a distributed computer-based collaborative learning system, *Proceedings of ED-TELECOM 96*, pp. 252-257.

Sun C. Chow C. (1996); Experiencing CORAL: Design and Implementation of Distant Co-operative Learning, *IEEE Transaction on Education*, Vol. 39,n. 3, 357-366.

WebCT. http://homebrew1.cs.ubc.ca/webct/.

2 A Virtual Secondary School Classroom on the Net

GIUSEPPE CHIAZZESE, CLAUDIA CORTOPASSI AND
MARIA RITA LAGANÀ, UNIVERSITY OF PISA

Abstract

This chapter presents an application level network service based on the TCP/IP reference model. Our service is made of both a new Co-operative Activity ConTrol Protocol (CACTP) and a new Application Program Interface. This service was used for the creation of an Interactive Multimedia Tele-learning Environment, which supports a virtual secondary school classroom where the children and the teacher join a synchronous class session in Internet/Intranet networks.

Introduction

Today advanced speed networks and multimedia technologies are transforming our planet into a global village. At the same time modern psychologists, following Vygotskyan's studies stress the creative strength of co-operation (Dillenberg et al. 1995). These elements together stimulate the creation of the co-operative tele-learning environment. Our work is in this context and while not forgetting the asynchronous component, we stress that children aged 9-12 need the synchronous component, which is missing in other educational environments (Turoff, 1995; Hiltz, 1995). Higher education is based on the concept of modules while children's education is based on the concept of the class.

In a real classroom we may distinguish two kinds of fundamental activities: the *synchronous activities* like reading, examinations, debates and the *asynchronous activities* like homework and personal re-elaboration. The first kind allows the unfolding of the lesson and the socialization with the other children while the second allows the re-elaboration of subjects considered in class and individual study.

The environment we propose transfers the didactic activity from the traditional classroom to a network learning space-environment removing the spatial restrictions but guaranteeing the typical socio-cognitive contacts of a traditional classroom. In our classroom, for example, the debates are not dominated by a restricted group of active pupils but all the children may express themselves freely in an ask-and-answer debate.

The one-to-one relation between teacher and e.g. a particularly intelligent child can be established without disturbing the usual lesson. All activities can be timed according to the children's capacities and organised in anonymous games that allow the timid child to find his role and to express himself.

We show in the next section the educational ideas underpinning our virtual environment, successively the architecture and the general characteristics of our software. We identify the components of our co-operative learning network in the model that we present in the fourth section and finally we show the scenarios and management of activities. We suggest the employment of these instruments also in local networks in order to improve the didactic quality.

Internet and Co-operative Learning

This section analyses the features of distance education versus school education and proposes an educational environment that improves on both by using Internet. The user has fundamentally two modes of communicating via Internet the *asynchronous* ("anytime/anywhere") mode when the sender and the receiver can connect at a different time and the *synchronous* mode when they are connected at the same-time by continuous connection. We observe that the users are distributed in different physical spaces and besides the human interactions are spontaneous, guided, and not guided, peer to peer, etc. Some questions are: " Must an educational network environment support synchronous or asynchronous communication?" – "Can these forms of distance interaction be used to improve learning environments?" The answers are linked to educational models.

Distance education is traditionally considered as a new way of delivering high quality lectures following an instruction plan. According to this model the student can organise his study and his learning time by himself so he may engage in effective understanding before going on with the course. In this model the interactions are limited: the teacher responds to students' demands (typically by email) and also the WWW is used as a store for remote courses and information.

A different vision of the learning process, related to socio-constructivist and socio-cultural theories, puts co-operation at the centre of this process. The thinking is not individual manipulation of mental objects but social sharing of them. Although some teachers prefer the instructional method, co-operative learning occurs in a spontaneous way in today school. Here students and groups of students learn by watching and working with a more skilled partner (typically the teacher), interact face to face sharing the goal of a problem solving strategy, and discuss an interesting issue among themselves and with the teachers. A real 'co-operative' teacher fosters conditions to involve the children in debates and activities that are meaningful for them. The educational results of Don Milani (DonMilani, 1970) that have changed the Italian school have stressed this kind of teacher role. The mechanisms of co-operative learning and the strength of the language in this process have been demonstrated by Vygotsky (Vygoskij, 1934). He assigned the teacher the role of meeting the student in the 'zone of proximal development' (which is close to our cognitive development) where we need help to carry out a task. The personalised elaboration is also important and must be combined with co-operative activity to create effective learning (Dillenberg et al. 1995).

Let us ask if it is possible to support in distance education the activities of a real school, without restricting classroom co-operation to the same physical space. Some researchers have proposed Internet-based tools for co-operative forms of learning (Turoff, 1995; Hiltz, 1995; Allegra et al. 1997): the virtual environment maintains the interactions related to mutual understanding and learning outcomes. These environments use asynchronous communication; where conferencing systems have been proposed (Handley et al. 1997) to support classroom-like experiences, they cover only a limited aspect of complex interactions. In the primary and secondary school the teacher role is very varied, the mental eagerness (the need to interact without delay) of her pupils must be exploited and capitalised on, friendship must be sustained and strengthened, and cultural differences must become part of the group's shared experience. In any case it is important not to allow the study-time to be prolonged.

So, in order to propose a virtual environment like the real school, we must first of all introduce synchronous communication. In this way we link teacher and pupils, situated in different places, in a common network session so as to allow real-time interactions. Furthermore we must implement the mechanisms to support both co-operative and individual activity carried out in the real school. But we can do more than a real school.

In our study we have observed a few serious problems in the real classroom: the discomfort the shyest boy feels at the sarcastic, whispered jokes, the know-all student's lack of turn-taking in answering questions, the respect for the leader who dominates the others. Sometimes the mutual regulation mechanism (for example when one has to justify why he does something) is not activated, due to the conceptual distance of the participants (real or created only for the pleasure of disturbing the lesson). The new technology enables us to overcome these problems and introduce a new educational model: the teacher plan effective classroom activities, giving him/her the role of firm mediator.

Figure 1 illustrates the idea of combining the positive characteristics of the two environments, distance and school education with all the mechanisms of co-operative learning in order to form a perfect school in the global village. We stress the features of this virtual environment: the space independence, the high quality lessons, the strong face-to-face-type social links, the freedom to intervene without disturbance, the granting of privacy and social correctness, too.

The virtual classroom that we propose in this chapter wishes to be an initial implementation of the new educational model that the new technologies make possible.

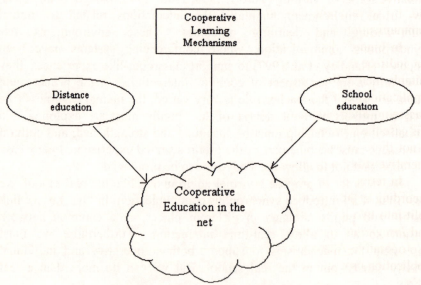

Figure 1 Ideal school on the net

Virtual Classroom Architecture

To describe our implementation we follow the metaphor of the secondary school. We build a classroom on the Net where the teacher can meet his pupils. During the hours of lessons, he/she alternates with his/her colleagues to carry out the single or co-operative activities of the children. The class-tests are in the teacher's drawer; the children find their diaries and notebooks on their desks. During the school time the teacher programs and improves single and co-operative didactic activities. Even if pupils can be checked by their teachers, now and then they can also share emotions and opinions with their network classmates, using a secret note. Because the users are present in remote sites, the software must ensure that they are not troubled by the distance dividing them. Therefore it keeps track of the composition of the class and any changes, and it evokes and amplifies the same physical-social contact as in the real classroom (I can choose whom I sit next to, whom to pat on the back and I can raise my hand).

This situation is implemented through a synchronous session. The software has been developed according to the client/server model (Comer et al. 1997). The network communication that we consider suitable for supporting our classroom is based on the one-to-many server communication model. The server is the teacher's workstation in the virtual classroom. Every student's client workstation communicates both directly with the teacher's server workstation by CACTP/TCP protocol message and, by server, with the workstation of the other students. We show the communication model in fig 2.

In Figure 2 the arrows for direct communication are black and those for indirect communication are dotted grey. We find this model more suitable than a direct communication between children, because the teacher (application) can easily monitor all information flows. The session in the classroom alternates with the session (always synchronous) at 'home'. In this case the server runs the unsupervised activities of the pupils; the teacher is not there to monitor. This environment is also a common room for co-operative study and play.

In terms of the general characteristics of our software, this is layered according to the Internet model (Comer, 1999) but with the application layer split into two levels (Fig 3). The upper level is the *Alunno (Student client)* and *Insegnante (Teacher server)* application and the lower level is CACTP (Co-operative Activity ConTrol Protocol) service that provides a network application protocol and an API for the upper level.

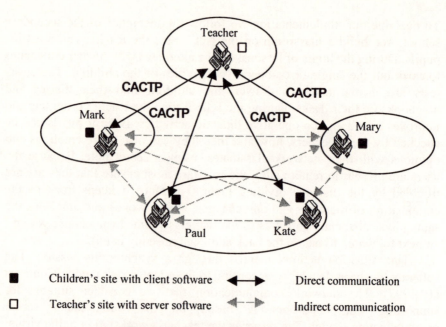

■	Children's site with client software	◀▬▶	Direct communication
□	Teacher's site with server software	◀▬ ▬▶	Indirect communication

Figure 2 Communication model

Up to this time there has been no commonly accepted service that incorporates all the facilities to support all the mechanisms of co-operation types (Shall, 1996). We have identified the functions needed for co-operation and we have used these in the upper layer where the client and server applications run. To obtain our goal, we have defined carefully the educational activities. They include free and controlled debate, presentation, questioning, exercises, group-work and even games. Moreover, we define the mechanisms for their development and control. It is convenient to distinguish three types of co-operation. The co-ordination regulates the actions between the participants using a synchronisation mechanism. The goal of collaboration is team production and so necessitates exchange mechanisms, floor control (Dommel et al. 1997) and sharing of the information. Finally the aim of co-decision is an accepted team decision and therefore needs voting mechanisms. In the next section we present our learning network co-operative model and we identify the facilities for this co-operative activity.

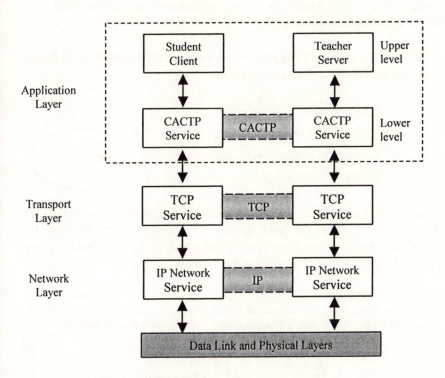

Figure 3 The application layer

Co-operative Learning Network Model

In this section we give a detailed description of the features of our virtual classroom. We present the organisational structure of the participants, the didactic activity which takes place in the classroom considering the complex exchanges, synchronisation and, in general, individual and group behaviour. We therefore use a model that describes the implemented features of the system. We identify the components of the teaching network in *commitment, nodes, relations* and *articulation* (Schäll, 1996). *Commitment* defines the type of activity that stimulates the session in class. It represents the input to the Co-operative Learning Network where the *nodes* are the individuals or workgroup units that participate in producing an object or making a decision; the *relations* are the interactions between nodes for sharing resources, knowledge and background and for collaborating in activities. The commitment in input determines the *articulation* into different jobs that are then assigned to the nodes.

The following components of our co-operative learning network provide an exhaustive description of the model.

- Didactic units (*commitment*)
- Child, Teacher, group (*nodes*)
- Classroom interaction (*relations*)
- Didactic Units articolation (*articulation*).

This conceptual model, shown in more detail in Figure 4, has been very useful in defining the facilities of the Co-operative Activity ConTrol Protocol. For every *network component* identified we have defined a group of protocol methods that characterize the network activity.

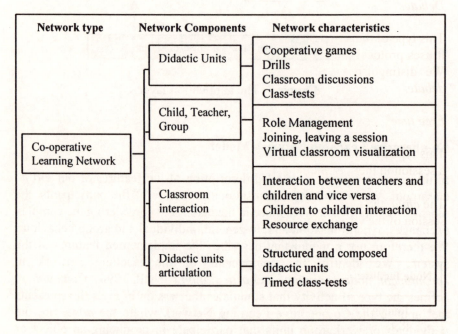

Figure 4 Co-operative learning network model

The teacher defines the input to the co-operative learning network through the didactic unit. We distinguish the following didactic units:

Didactic Units

- Cooperative games, Drills, Class-tests
- Debates
- Free time

Co-operative games, drills, class-tests

At the moment we have used the HTML format for these didactic units, both because this is a very suitable standard for the distribution of data in the network and because it possesses the multimedia capability that is needed in secondary school classrooms.

Debates

This type of didactic unit does not require the production of a document, but it uses protocol methods for the textual communication within the session. We distinguish *classroom discussion* (with teacher control) from *free debate.*

Free time

This type of "didactic unit" allows the pupils to engage in free activity with a session in the "common room".

The *child*, the *teacher* and the *group* are "living" entities of the synchronous session of the virtual classroom. They take part in the didactic activities.

Node facilities

- Joining, Leaving a session and node visualization
- Roles and workgroup management

Joining, leaving a session and nodes visualization

The server responds to the participation request of the clients by granting or refusing admittance. A classroom session starts with the teacher entering the classroom and telling the children his name and the subject of his lesson. The beginning and the end of the classroom activities are marked by the ringing of a bell.

The client supports the facilities for joining or leaving a session. Any new connection creates a new TCP/IP communication channel between the pupil and the teacher. The service records and updates the pupils' attendances and absences. Any change of teacher or subject is communicated to the nodes. So the user application can visualise the class composition: all the participants can see it for the whole time they are connected to the session. The exit of a teacher from the classroom delivers the commitment *free time*.

Roles and workgroup management

The service may assign the role of supervisor to the teacher so he can control the activity in the class. He may also prevent a pupil from sending/receiving messages to/from others pupils and even expel him from the session. These functions put a stop to incorrect behaviour within the classroom if other attempts prove ineffective. Only when the time (established by the teacher) of a suspension comes to an end will the pupil be able to rejoin the session.

The service supports various mechanisms for workgroup management: opening and monitoring the voting process to elect group leaders, listing the candidates, collecting, counting and sending the votes. It communicates the list of group leaders elected to all nodes.

The leader role gives the pupils permission to form workgroups through a turn taking mechanism, and to send the workgroup results to the teacher. The group formations are communicated to the whole class.

The classroom interaction component enables the pupils to attend the virtual classroom and to interact through textual communication and exchange of resources:

Classroom interaction facilities

- Communication between participants
- Rules for conducting class discussions
- Monitoring the attention level

Communication between the nodes

The CACTP service supports three kinds of communication: open discussion, group-communication (within a group or between groups) and private communication. Moreover it integrates the ftp service for the distribution and exchange of multimedia resources. In order to enable the teacher to monitor the pupils, we have included a buffer area in his computer to transfer resources. The protocol implements the transfer in two steps. The CACTP client service of the sender pupil opens an ftp session and orders the ftp server to move the resource into the exchange area of the teacher's remote computer. As soon as the transfer has been completed, it closes the ftp session and sends a message to the receiver's CACTP client with details of the resource. Then the receiver's CACTP client service informs the pupil. If the pupil decides to acquire the resource immediately, the receiver's CACTP client service opens a session to transfer the resource from the teacher's computer.

Rules for class discussion

The service allows a pupil to book his turn to speak in a polite manner by raising his hand. His request is passed on through the protocol to the teacher who then allows the pupil to take part in the discussion.

Monitoring attention level

During a teaching period the service can inform the teacher of the number of exchanges taking place between the various network classmates. In this way he can redirect the attention of pupils who are distracted.

Didactic Units articulation

- Selection of didactic units and distribution of these to the nodes
- Type of didactic activity: individual, group work, anonymous
- Timing of a classroom task
- Sending work to the teacher

Selection and distribution of the didactic units

Figure 5 shows the process and the components involved in the distribution process of a didactic unit to the pupils. In this figure we have considered the case where two students and a teacher take part in a session. The process of sending a didactic unit follows a series of steps governed by the interactions between the teacher and students. Through the CACTP service the student receive a message that tells them the file name of the exercise chosen by the teacher. If the user asks the CACTP service to see the didactic unit, the service opens a transparent session with an ftp server and begins to transfer the didactic unit to the pupils' computers. When transfer is completed the CACTP service closes the ftp session.

The protocol ensures that the interactions between nodes take place according to the type of activity specified by the teacher.

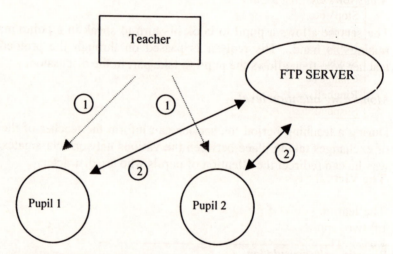

1. Message of the arrival of a didactic unit from the teacher server.
2. Transparent ftp session for the transfer of the didactic unit.

Figure 5 Distribution process of a didactic unit to the pupils

Timing controls of classroom tasks

The protocol specifies the time allowed for class activities.

Sending work to the teacher

The service provides facilities for sending 'exercise books' to the teacher with the solutions to the exercises. These 'exercise books' are returned with the corrections and the teacher's mark. All API calls are listed in Table 1:

CreateSession	SendMsgToGroup
CloseSession	SendMsgToPartner
JoiningSession	SendMsgToClassroom
LeavingSession	SendExercise
NewVote	SendSolution
StopVote	ConnectTo Resource Server
TurnOfChoice	DisconnectFromResourceServer
NewGroup	GetResourceFrom
SendMsgToTeacher	PutResourceTo
ChangeTeacher	PuttingUpHand
Ringbell	PuttingDownHand
SuspendStudent	GiveSpeech

Table 1 The API methods

The Virtual Secondary School Classroom

The learning environment prototype that uses the CACTP service consists of two applications that we have developed: *Pupil* client and *Teacher server*. The Client environment is shown in Fig. 6.

On the toolbar there are the buttons that allow the user to choose the activities. To connect to the server the user writes his or her name in the Connection Area; they disconnect by clicking the appropriate button.

To integrate local and remote space our User Interface makes use of five work scenarios:

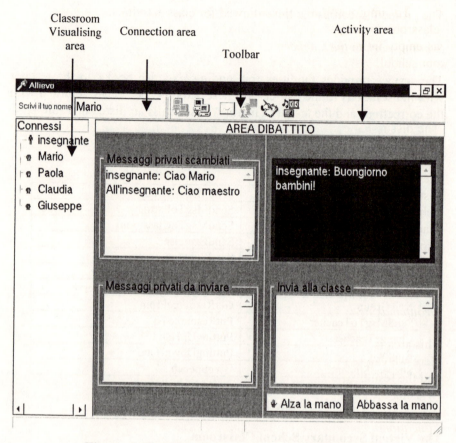

Figure 6 The Virtual Secondary School Classroom

Classroom visualization

This area makes the students aware of the make-up of the class and of their role at that moment. In our present implementation each pupil is represented by a head-shaped icon with his name written next to it. A hand raised next to the pupil's icon indicates his intention to speak in the debate; a red sign next to a friend's icon means communication with him is not allowed (when there is an exercise to do, for example); a flashing pen tells the pupil that an exercise is arriving, the teacher icon next to his icon lets him know that at that moment his is being monitored. For timed activities we use an egg timer.

To improve this interface we propose displaying a map of the classroom with the teacher's and students' desks, which can then be shown as empty to indicate absentees. A clock on the wall will show the time in our school.

Discussion area

The discussion area (shown in Figure 6) makes it possible to participate in both private (individual explanations, exchange of personal ideas) and class conversation (collective explanations, question and answer sessions). A message written in the space reserved for class communication is then visualised on the 'blackboard' with the sender's name. If the controlled debate mode has been activated, the discussion is displayed on the teacher's blackboard for as long as she feels it is necessary (so everyone has time to express his ideas on a complex subject without being conditioned by other opinions). Finally, the private message area is reserved for personal communication.

Group making area

This area is used for electing group-leaders and then for forming the groups. Here we can see the number of groups to be formed, the list of candidates and the results of the election. The votes are cast and the groups are formed by using the mouse.

Educational activities

Activities in this area can be carried out in the presence of the teacher, who 'walks' around the classroom to monitor the didactic activity, or without the teacher. Here the student can use his diary and notebook, where he practises and also records the resources that he accepts from his companions. The interface uses the functions of the CACTP service to indicate the presence of an exercise or task, to transfer the didactic unit to the student's computer and to hand back the student's work to the teacher. In the case of a class task it monitors who is allowed to exchange messages and whether the task is handed in at the end of the lesson.

Multimedia resource exchange area

This area makes it possible to exchange and visualise resources: images, sounds, video clips. The pupil chooses the receiver and the resource to be sent. The user's interface, using the appropriate CACTP services, transfers the resources, indicating to the receiver that it is doing so, in order that they can give approve the process. The resources not used at that moment are saved and can be accessed later.

Conclusion

In this work we have defined and implemented a new network application service (CACTP protocol and interface API) for co-operative learning activity control in real-time environment that uses a TCP/IP transport level communication protocol. All the facilities of the Co-operative Activity ConTrol Protocol are encapsulated in a unique service that has been used for the implementation of user applications for our virtual classroom environment.

This environment gives an original atmosphere to the method of learning because it allows both synchronous and asynchronous activities. It enhances the group, the socialization of the children, but at the same time it allows them to reflect on their own. The system may be used within the four walls of an average classroom with a link to, say, a child who is ill at home. Or perhaps a link may be needed to the teacher who is currently not present at school due to unforeseen circumstances. The virtual school, which we are proposing, has, like every piece of software, only potential characteristics: just as an empty classroom with desks and chairs awaits a teacher and pupils to make it come alive. Our class has had a brief trial within the secondary school of Capannori (Lucca-Italy) but it still has to be experimented fully. We believe that schools in the millennium will profit from tools similar to ours and that the technological 'robot teacher' will not succeed, because he lacks the interpersonal relationships which the new tools allow us to maintain.

References

Allegra M. Chifari A. Fulantelli G. Ottaviano S. (1997); An On Line Cooperative Learning Environment *Canadian Journal of Education Communication* Vol 26, n. 2.

Comer D. Stevens D. (1997); *Internetworking with TCP/IP Volume III: Client-Server Programming and Applications*, Prentice-Hall International, Inc.

Comer D. (1999); *Computer networks and Internets*, Prentice-Hall International, Inc.

Dillenberg P. and Schneider D. (1995); Collaborative Learning in the Internet, *Proceedings, Fourth Int. Conference on Computer Assisted Instruction*, Taiwan.

Dommel P. Garcia-Luna-Aceves J.J. (1997); Floor Control for Multimedia Conferencing and Collaboration in *ACM Journal on MM Sys* Vol 5, n. 1,gennaio.

DonMilani (1970); *Lettere di Don Lorenzo Milani priore di Barbiana*, Gesualdi Michele (Editor), Mondadori Press.

Grebner R. (1997); Use of instructinal material in universal teleteaching environments, *Computer Networks and ISDN systems*. n. 29.

Handley M. et al. The Internet Multimedia Conferencing Architecture, *Internet draft, IETF, draft-ietf-mmusic-confarc-00.txt*.

Hilt V. and Werner G. (1997); A Model for Collaborative Services in Distributed Learning Environments, *LNCS* 1309 pp. 364-375.

Hiltz S.R. (1995); Teaching in a virtual classroom, *International Conference on Computer Assisted Instruction* ICCAI 95
  http://www.njit.edu/njIT/Department/CCCC/VC/Papers/.

Schäll T. (1996); Workflow Management Systems for Process Organizations, *Lecture Notes in Computer Science*, Vol 1096.

Turoff M. (1995); Designing a Virtual Classroom, *International Conference on Computer Assisted Instruction* ICCAI 95
  http://www.njit.edu/njIT/Department/CCCC/VC/Papers/.

Vygoskij S.L. (1934); Myslenie i rec'. Psichologiceskie issledovanija, *Gosudarstvennoe Social'no-Ekonomiceskoe Izdatel'stvo*, Moskva-Leningrad, 1934.

3 The Virtual Student: User Embodiment in Virtual Learning Environments

MARC FABRI AND MICHAEL GERHARD
AXIS - FOR INFORMATION ON VISUAL ARTS, LEEDS, UK

Abstract

As virtual universities become widely deployed, their students are likely to want to 'attend' virtual tutorials and seminars, take part in collaborative learning, and carry their identity, belongings, moods, and preferences with them. Their educational experience is likely to be enhanced if they can interact with their virtual learning environment and with each other in an intelligent and 'natural' way, and can communicate and collaborate synchronously as well as asynchronously; in other words, in their presence and absence respectively.

This chapter investigates the usability of three-dimensional, multi-user Virtual Learning Environments (VLEs) for such educational purposes. A brief overview of the underlying technology and its relevance for education are provided. Based on the theory of cognitive immersion, the significance of emotionally expressive avatars in facilitating the process of human communication and interaction is discussed. As a result of this discussion, the use of animated agents for achieving a permanent virtual presence of students in VLEs is proposed.

Introduction

Life-long learning and training-on-the-job is of increasing importance in today's society. The World Wide Web is considered likely to change the face of the learning discipline fundamentally. It embodies a convergence of the previously separate technologies and industries of computing, telecommunications, and television (Bates 1998). The collaborative features of the WWW can enable learners and tutors to overcome spatial distances and work together more efficiently (Hobbs and Taylor 1996). Learners can meet *virtually*, exchanging their ideas and resources, discussing their educational concerns with, and seeking advice from, their tutors. Learning can now be experienced in Web-based, 3-dimensional, virtual worlds, where participants are represented by their avatars.

In this chapter, we focus on the interface aspects of such a virtual learning environment (VLE) with particular regard to user representation and perceptions of interlocutors within the same virtual world. We argue for the use of persistent and expressive user embodiments in VLE's, outline our prototypes, and discuss plans for our experimental research.

The Role of Interaction in Education

Interaction is of key importance for the process of learning. Moore (1993) identifies three general types of interaction in education, characterised by interaction taking place:
- between student and learning content
- between student and teacher
- between student and fellow student.

The interaction between student and learning content is well researched. Frameworks exist for analysing educational media in terms of how they support the teaching-learning process and the different modes of learning (cf. Laurillard 1993).

The student-teacher interaction as well as the student-student interaction can be described as communication between the participants in the teaching-learning process. The importance of these human-to-human types of interaction for the process of learning has been widely acknowledged (Laurillard 1993, Garrison 1993, Moore 1993). In particular, these types of interaction allow mutual reflection on actions and problem solutions, motivation and stimulation as well as assessment and control of progress. Laurillard (1995) proposes a comprehensive model for the process of learning through interaction and reflection, referred to as the 'guided discovery approach'.

Learning through guided discovery

The model of learning through guided discovery is widely valued in the academic community. It promotes active reflection on the side of both the student and the teacher, and integrates the student's experiential and conceptual knowledge of the learning subject. Figure 1 illustrates the cyclic process of guided discovery.

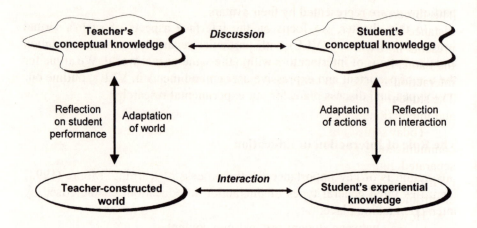

Figure 1 Modes of learning: Learning through guided discovery
(Laurillard 1995)

The model is based on the following four entities:

- the teacher's conceptual knowledge of learning material and desired outcomes

- the student's conceptual knowledge of the learning material in general

- the student's experiential knowledge of the learning environment

- the learning environment constructed by the teacher.

By interacting with the teacher constructed learning environment, the student gains experiential knowledge of the material presented. When subsequently reflecting on the interaction, the student builds up their conceptual knowledge of the learning domain in general. At the same time, the teacher reflects on student performance and adapts the learning environment accordingly.

In the following paragraphs, we will apply the guided discovery approach to the process of learning in a virtual learning environment. We will show that reflection and adaptation are possible and that the opportunities for a teacher to create a stimulating learning environment are actually enriched due to the highly interactive nature of the medium VLE.

Interaction in distance learning systems

The three interaction paradigms retain their validity when applied to the distance learning discipline. However, whilst the student-content interaction presents no extra difficulty for distance as opposed to proximate learning, the same is not true of the remaining two paradigms. Human-to-human interaction is often difficult and limited in distance learning programmes. The student typically has to work with far less guiding help from the teacher and interactions with fellow students are rather limited (Rowntree 1993).

Today's distance learning programmes already make use of various communication technologies to enable communication between spatially separated tutors and learners, and between learners and fellow learners (Wilson and Whitelock 1998). These technologies include telephony, electronic mail, text-based chat, or video-conferencing systems.

However, when communicating through these media, we often lose the emotional context, and the ability to express our emotional state in the way we are accustomed to in face-to-face conversations. When using text-based tools, important indicators like accentuation, emotion, change of emotion and intonation are difficult to mediate (Ødegård 1993). Audio conferencing tools, for example the telephone network, can ease some of these difficulties but lack ways to mediate non-verbal means of communication such as facial expressions or gesture, channels that play an important role in human interaction. Video conferencing can alleviate some of the shortcomings concerning non-verbal communication. However, it has been observed that due to the non-immersive character of video-based interfaces, the conversational thread during meetings can easily break down when people are distracted by external influences, or have to handle electronically shared data (McShea et al 1997).

We are therefore conducting research into a potentially useful alternative, namely the use of multi-user virtual reality systems as communication and collaboration tools for distance learning purposes. The following paragraph gives a brief overview of this technology and outlines the potential benefits for educational applications.

Virtual Learning Environments – a new educational paradigm

Technology overview

A virtual environment (VE) is an interactive simulation of 3-dimensional structures in a virtual world. VEs support natural aspects of human perception by extending visual information in three spatial dimensions. A central component of any VE system is the ability to interact by direct manipulation (Mann and Mon-Williams 1996).

Collaborative Virtual Environments (CVEs) are networked, multi-user, virtual environments. The user-interface of a CVE must allow engagement not only with objects but, additionally, communication with other users. In fact, CVEs actively seek to support human-human communication and collaboration in addition to human-machine interaction. The participants are *virtually* in the same shared virtual world and can interact with it, and with each other. A virtual user embodiment, known as *avatar*, represents the user in the virtual environment.

As an example, Figure 2 shows a screenshot from Blaxxun's ColonyCity, an online community accessible via the World Wide Web (see Blaxxun 1999).

Figure 2 Collaborative virtual environment with various user embodiments

The avatar usually resembles a humanoid shape and has identifying attributes, enabling the user to carry their identity, moods, and preferences with them, recognisable by the other inhabitants of the virtual world. Since each avatar is both part of the perceived environment and represents the user that is doing the perceiving (Slater and Wilbur 1997), CVEs potentially offer a high level of mutual awareness. A detailed discussion of potential avatar characteristics is provided later in this chapter.

Furthermore, due to the highly visual and stimulating nature of CVEs, users are likely to be actively engaged in interaction with the virtual world and with other inhabitants. It has been argued that this high-level interactivity, where the users' senses are engaged in the action and they 'feel' they are participating, is an essential factor of the learning process (Stoney and Wild 1998).

Virtual environments for distance learning

In educational CVEs, spatially separated learners are able to work together in the same virtual space, to exchange ideas and learning materials, and to discuss their educational concerns with, and seek advice from, a tutor (Fabri 1998).

We call such an educational CVE system a Virtual Learning Environment (VLE). In a VLE, students can 'attend' virtual tutorials and seminars, take part in collaborative learning, and can carry their identity, belongings, moods, and preferences with them. Their educational experience is likely to be enhanced if they can interact with the environment and with each other in an intelligent and natural way. Further, Hobbs and Taylor (1998) believe that VLEs may bring back some of the social intercourse of 'campus' life that is usually lost in distance education.

Virtual Learning Environments allow the effective integration of learning resources and foster intuitive ways of information visualisation and access. Some educational applications can directly benefit from breaking the bounds of two-dimensional representation because of their natural affinity with 3D-objects, e.g. medical training, architectural visualisation, flight simulation, and molecular models. For existing applications see (Rosenblum 1997, Mitchell 1997).

Indeed, VLEs can have wide-ranging educational benefits by offering the student a stimulating shared learning space in which various forms of interaction and collaboration methods are available. The environment acts as a sophisticated communication tool, enabling spatially separated learners to overcome the distance and work together effectively and efficiently. This can be of advantage in disciplines where the subject matter is predominantly theoretical and controversial, such as in social science or humanities (see Gibbs and Henry 1996).

Students working and collaborating in a VLE may create tools or objects (e.g. work aids, idea prototypes, discussion maps) that everyone uses, and therefore contribute towards a common goal. There is good evidence that in such learning environments, less well qualified students can learn from the better qualified, and the latter can also gain valuable interaction skills (O'Malley 1995).

Guided discovery in VLEs

Figures 3 and 4 illustrate the process of learning through guided discovery within a VLE. As in the traditional model, the learning content in the virtual world is usually teacher constructed. In the VLE, however, interaction with the content as well as communication with other participants is avatar-mediated.

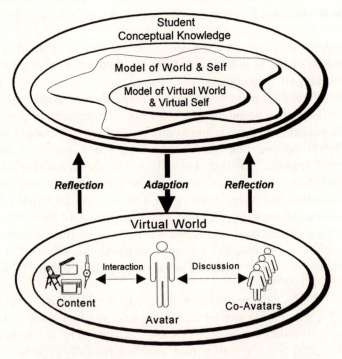

Figure 3 Student's perspective of learning in a VLE

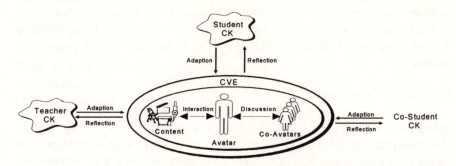

Figure 4 Collaborative learning through 'guided discovery' in a VLE
(CK=Conceptual Knowledge)

By reflecting on the content as well as on student-teacher and student-student discussions within the VLE, the student builds up a model of the virtual world. In addition, the student develops their awareness of 'virtual self' within the learning environment.

Actions and expectations are influenced by, and adapted to, the environment, and the experiential model becomes part of the student's conceptual knowledge. Figure 4 illustrates how teacher, student, and fellow students are interconnected within the VLE.

In this scenario, the avatar is the primary interaction mechanism for operating within the virtual learning environment. Firstly, it enables the participants to be aware of, and relate to, each other. Secondly, it potentially enables the learner to express their current emotional state and their ability to interact and communicate. Thirdly, it provides the other participants with visual clues about a particular user's current actions and about the effects these actions have on the learning environment.

Cognitive Aspects of Immersion

It is claimed that what distinguishes CVE technology in general, and VLEs in particular, from preceding technologies is the sense of immediacy and control created by immersion. The inhabitant potentially develops a sense of presence, or the feeling of actually 'being there' (Psotka 1995). The engagement and excitement that is part of the VE phenomenon is an obvious benefit of immersion that can be brought to education and training applications (Bricken and Byrne 1993).

Considering immersion as potentially the 'key added value' of virtual environments, researchers have only just begun to analyse what immersion is, what cognitive variables are connected to immersion, how it is generated in multi-user virtual environments, and what its benefits for education and training are.

The degree of immersion

Based on the theory of *Distal Attribution* (Loomis 1992), Tromp (1995) identifies four variables to the experience, and the degree of immersion (see Figure 5). Tromp states that the degree of immersion that a user will be able to experience is basically dependent on two factors:

- the quality of the avatars and interactivity, which are characteristics of the virtual environment, and
- the ability to become absorbed in the activity and the quantity of experience with the virtual world, both of which are user characteristics.

Figure 5 shows the dependencies of these factors. Tromp refers to the subjective feeling of immersion that emerges as *Cognitive Immersion*, and it is argued that for the degree of cognitive immersion a person feels, the respective person's own attitudes are more important than the characteristics of the interface (Tromp 1995).

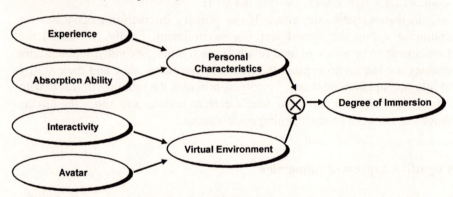

Figure 5 Model for the theory of Cognitive Immersion (Tromp 1995)

People can become cognitively immersed in a movie, a book, and the spontaneous memory of a situation in the past. Stimulated in this way, our senses can utilise information to generate and elaborate sensations and thereby arouse a feeling of being physically present in the virtual environment. The environment specified by the displays should be considered as places visited, people met, situations experienced, rather than as images seen.

Ellis (1995) points out that this sense of physical reality is a consequence of internal processing rather than being something that is developed only from the immediate sensory information we receive. Ultimately, the reality perceived could be considered as being 'made' in the mind of the perceiver rather than by the device that initially creates the stimuli.

Perceiving realism or reality?

In this context, we find it important to distinguish between the perception of *realism* and the perception of *reality*. *Realism* can be perceived when the environment simulates the real world, i.e. it offers an illusion based on the real world that the user then accepts as being the real world, or at least a good replica. We define perceiving *reality* as *experiencing* a situation in the virtual environment, no matter how abstract the environment might be, or if the situation would be impossible in the real world. The ultimate aim is not to simulate the real world, but to enable a stimulating experience.

Interestingly, many virtual reality systems intend to simulate the real world and its sensory feedback as accurately as possible. Realism is often seen as the main requirement for participants to accept the virtual environment and have the sense of 'being there', of being immersed in it (see Capin et al 1997, Slater and Usoh 1994). However, realism might not generally be the best approach, and, as Carr (1995) points out, informed deviation from realistic patterns of information may allow virtual reality to communicate more effectively than reality itself. As pointed out earlier, the degree to which a user feels present, or immersed, in a virtual world depends on the person's own attitudes, and not in the first place on the technology (Tromp 1995). It is the willingness to accept the stimulant offered by some medium as real that creates a state of mental absorption, or cognitive immersion.

Applied to communication and interaction in a VLE, these arguments suggest that whilst our senses, in this case primarily the visual sensory system, do need a certain stimulation and continuous feedback from the interface to sustain the state of cognitive immersion, the stimuli do not have to be a detailed replica of the real world. There is evidence that approaches aiming to reproduce for example the detailed physics of human movement may in fact be unnecessary (Benford et al 1995). Instead, a more abstract approach, reflecting representation issues in simple or unusual ways, may be more appropriate and supportive to perception and cognition (Godenschweger et al 1997).

We are taking this into account when we design avatars for our own experimental learning environments, particularly for the visualisation of a user's emotional state. We argue that the purposeful use of simple, but succinct visual communication metaphors in VLEs is potentially a highly effective (and efficient) way to create an atmosphere resembling face-to-face communication that encourages the user to feel immersed in the virtual environment. For a more detailed discussion of the cognitive processes taking place when interacting with and within a virtual environment, see Fabri et al 1999.

User Embodiment in VLEs

The fact of being represented by a virtual embodiment is generally seen as highly significant for the psychological phenomenon of presence in collaborative virtual environments (Benford et al 1995, Slater and Usoh 1994). This influence is crucial since presence is seen as an important factor for effectively performing in those environments (Witmer and Singer 1998). Aspects relevant to user embodiment within VLEs, and in particular the concepts of avatar and agent technologies, will now be outlined followed by a discussion of the potential benefits of a hybrid system, combining these two concepts.

Avatars
An avatar may be defined as:

> "The embodiment, or representation, of a user's awareness and identity within a multi-user computer environment." (Gerhard and Moore 1998)

Avatars have a number of potential characteristics, which are outlined in the following sections.

Identity Avatars provide a way for other users to better understand the intended persona of the underlying user, the user's identity. By equipping the avatar with certain visual characteristics, the user can influence their virtual identity.

Presence It is held that avatars help establishing a form of self-location, a sense of presence. Typically, the embodiment is the centre of self in the virtual world. Since each avatar is also perceivable by the other inhabitants, it engenders a feeling of mutual awareness, the sense of co-presence.

Subordination Avatars also imply subordination, i.e. being under the direct control of the user, without having significant control over their own actions and internal state. However, when combined with agent technology, avatars can become partly or fully autonomous and the level of subordination varies (Gerhard and Moore 1998).

Authority Avatars generally act with the authority of the user. Again, this can vary with the degree of autonomy granted by the agent logic.

Social facilitation Avatars can provide social facilitation by giving a proxy for human communication and by facilitating interaction. The avatar can provide direct feedback about one particular users' actions, attentive state, interaction abilities, and current emotional state, to the other inhabitants (Fabri and Hobbs 1998).

In the following paragraphs, we will investigate some of these characteristics in detail. *Presence and Co-Presence* will look at the psychological and social aspects of being aware of oneself and others in a VLE. Related to this, *The Persistent Avatar* introduces agent technology to create a state of continuous user presence in virtual environments. Finally, *The Expressive Avatar* explores ways to give avatars an emotional state.

Presence and co-presence

When information about an environment is presented to an individual, that individual may have the sense of being present in that environment to a greater or lesser extent. *Presence* is the effect of immersion and refers to the specific sense of self-location in an environment, engendered by the user embodiment. It has been argued that there is an inherent connection between the degree of presence and the virtual body (Slater and Usoh 1994, Slater et al 1998).

Co-presence in turn describes the awareness of the existence of others within an environment. We not only identify with our own body, but we also recognise the existence of others through their bodies. In addition to the self-location effect an avatar engenders for the user that controls it, avatars can provide presence and support social facilitation of all participants within a collaborative virtual environment.

There has been little research into the psychological dimensions of co-presence and its relation to the process of cognitive immersion. However, Huxor (1998) found evidence that if members of a group do not feel co-present, there is a lack of community feeling between them and this can have detrimental effects on their performance.

In the light of this, we see a clear need for co-presence within VLEs to enable learners to collaborate and co-operate effectively. To create, and more importantly to sustain something like 'campus-feeling', we propose the permanent representation of students and teachers in virtual learning environments. Continuous avatar presence, or presence-in-absence, would give all participants a persistent proxy for communication and collaboration, at any time (Gerhard and Moore 1998).

The persistent avatar

The idea of a persistent avatar and its implications are now discussed under the following sections.

The agent takes over Software agents are meant to carry out tasks for the user and serve as another layer of mediation within the system (Maes 1995). In search of a universal definition, Franklin and Graesser (1996) propose several properties for software agents: reactive, autonomous, goal-oriented, temporally continuous, communicative, able to learn, flexible. Thus, agents not only act simply in response to the environment, but they can also be pro-active and purposeful, and they can exercise control over their own actions to a certain predefined degree. In a virtual environment, they could communicate with other agents and avatars. Agents can have a believable personality and emotional state, and mediate this via an avatar.

By applying artificial intelligence technology, such as expert systems, neural networks, and genetic algorithms, avatars can be adaptive and can learn. Instead of scripted actions, their behaviour can be based on their previous experience. Agents may turn out to be very beneficial for successful interaction and learning in CVEs, and may play an important role in respect of the psychological phenomena of immersion and presence discussed earlier.

This clearly has implications on some of the avatar characteristics listed earlier. When agent technology is being introduced, *subordination* and *authority* are no longer absolute characteristics but vary in their degree, depending on the quality and tasks of the agent. Equally, *social facilitation* provided by some software agent and mediated via an avatar does not necessarily reflect the intentions of an underlying user. There has been little research to date into how the introduction of agent technology changes the social aspects of collaborative virtual environments, but it can be expected to be a growing area of research in the near future.

Continuous presence Distant learners are typically working responsibly, at their own pace and time, without having to adapt their daily routine to an imposed learning schedule. This is not only considered good practice, but also a declared objective of the open, learner-centred approach to distant education (Rowntree 1993). However, since each student is working independently, teachers and fellow students might not be available for the discussion of, and reflection on, ideas and educational concerns.

Therefore, in a CVE for distance learning, the need for both synchronous and asynchronous forms of communication and collaboration arises. We argue that continuous intelligent presence of all participants involved in the teaching-learning process would be beneficial in such environments. A hybrid avatar/agent model is seen as a potential means of achieving this form of permanent presence in CVEs (Gerhard 1997). In the absence of the underlying user, the avatar can function as an intelligent agent, perceiving and responding within the environment, giving, receiving, and filtering information in order to fulfil a predefined task. Maes speculates on the future role of software agents:

> "Information overload is the problem that agents alone can solve.
> Users are increasingly dealing with vast amounts of information that is
> unstructured and very dynamic. In order to keep track of everything,
> and in order to find the information relevant to them, they will have to
> use software that knows their interests and can act on their behalf."
> (Maes 1997)

The autonomous character of agents and the subordinated character of avatars might seem to be contradictory. However, considering that a hybrid avatar/agent model can represent the user in presence as well as absence, it is not inherently paradoxical. With the user being present, the avatar operates under direct control, whereas with the user being absent, the avatar, extended with agent technology, can exercise control over its own interactions with other users and the environment. Intelligent agent technology allows the user to customise the avatar's behaviour for the times of absence and therefore influences the avatar's operations towards a predefined learning goal.

The expressive avatar

Natural human communication is based on speech, facial expressions and gestures. While speech is the most obvious instrument for mediating our ideas, thoughts and emotions, social intercourse also depends heavily on the actions, postures, movements and expressions of the talking body (Morris et al 1979). Social psychologists argue that more than 65% of the information exchanged during a person-to-person conversation is carried on the non-verbal band (Morris et al 1979, Knapp 1978). Therefore, we suggest that these non-verbal means of communication should be supported within a collaborative virtual environment in some way.

Non-verbal means of expression are also important in the educational environment, for the facilitation of interaction between tutor and learner, as well as between fellow learners (Knapp 1978). Acceptance and understanding of ideas and feelings, encouraging and criticising, silence and questioning - all involve non-verbal elements of interaction and it can be argued that computer-based educational technologies ought to emulate this.

Non-verbal communication channels   There are various channels for non-verbal communication (NVC), such as the face, gaze, gesture, or body posture. However, the most immediate indicator for the emotional state of a person is the face (Knapp 1978). It reflects interpersonal attitudes, provides feedback on the comments of others, and is regarded as the primary source of information next to human speech. For these reasons, humans naturally pay a great deal of attention to the messages they receive from the faces of others.

Considerable research has shown that there are six universal emotions, which can be accurately communicated by facial expressions:

1. Surprise	4. Anger
2. Fear	5. Happiness
3. Disgust	6. Sadness

It is held that these six emotions have an innate physiological basis and a clear meaning across cultures (cf. Ekman and Friesen 1978, Argyle 1994, Zebrowitz 1997).

Another strong indicator for emotion, and particularly attitude, is body posture. By taking on certain postures, people can send clear signals regarding their current willingness and ability to engage in social interaction (Argyle 1988). Such attitude postures are often combined with hand and arm gestures. There is evidence that, similar to facial expressions, certain postures have a clear meaning across cultures too (Argyle 1988). These include welcoming, rejection, incomprehension, and a posture signalling attention.

In our experimental work, we are investigating the use of simple, but distinctive visual clues to mediate the emotional state of a VLE user (see Figure 6). We focus particularly on those NVC channels that mediate emotions and attitudes, as these factors are essential to human social interaction (Argyle 1988, Dittrich et al 1996). In fact, it is held that, where communication of changing moods and emotional states is concerned, nonverbal information is far more important than verbal information (Morris et al 1979).

Emotion recognition The expression of emotion, in the face or through the body, is seen as being part of a wider system of natural human communication that has evolved to facilitate social life (Argyle 1988). The psychologist Neisser (1976) argues that cognitive schemata for physiognomic perception exist to pick up the expressive signals offered by members of our own species, and that these schemata could be innate. In accordance with Neisser's theory, Bassili (1978, 1979) and later Dittrich (1993, 1996) found clear indications for a schemata-based processing of visual stimuli that enable us to recognise facial expressions and body motion even in poor visual conditions, from very few stimuli. This naturally-acquired human skill of being able to 'read' emotions from signals displayed by the body is considered as being highly beneficial to communication in virtual learning environments. We argue that an emotionally expressive user embodiment can aid the communication process between all participants in the learning process, and provide information that would otherwise be difficult to mediate. Further, we propose that although the user embodiment does not have to be a realistic and accurate representation of the real world physiognomy, it should resemble the visual characteristics of a humanoid shape to enable the recognition of emotion and social attitude.

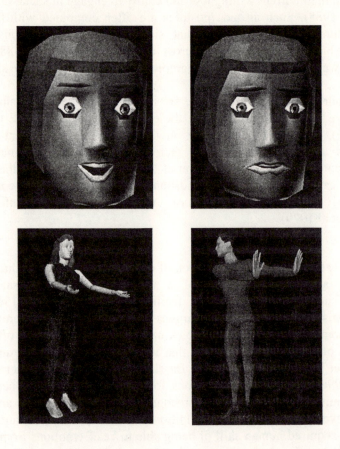

Figure 6 Surprise and sadness face, welcoming and rejection posture

Visualising the user's state The human body consists of a number of segments (such as the forearm, hand and foot) that are connected to each other by joints (such as the elbow, wrist and ankle). In order to control the appearance and to animate gestures of a humanoid avatar in a virtual environment, an application needs to obtain access to these joints and alter the joint angles (Roehl 1998).

There are three approaches to the problem of capturing and displaying nonverbal means of expression of students and teachers in a VLE through their avatars (Capin et al 1997):

-   Directly controlled: Movements of the user's face and body are captured and the avatar is modified directly, ideally in real-time, via virtual 'strings' like a marionette, cf. (Pandzic et al 1994)

-   User-guided: The user guides the virtual human by defining tasks and movements to perform and the virtual 'strings' are controlled via a secondary device, which could be a mouse or keyboard, cf. (Capin et al 1997, Fabri and Hobbs 1998)

-   Autonomous: The virtual human is assumed to have an internal state that depends on its goals and sensor information from the environment. The controlling user modifies this state, e.g. re-defines goals and starts tasks, cf. (Gerhard et al 1999, Johnson et al 1998).

Our work is concerned with a control mechanism that lies somewhere between the user-guided and the autonomous approach. We consider the purposeful use of higher-level visualisation metaphors as an efficient and effective way of expressing a user's state. This can be the emotional state, the degree of attention, or the spatial orientation of the user. For example, instead of faithfully visualising limb and face movements of an angry user, rage could be visualised by a red-faced avatar with steam coming out of the ears.

To express emotion on the virtual face, we use the most distinctive appearances of the six emotion categories. Preliminary findings suggest that there is a psychological basis for recognising these emotions even from a small number of facial clues. Our example head uses the following set of parameters to change the facial expression:

The virtual head shown in Figure 7 features all moveable parts in neutral position. The happiness expression on the left, for example, is constructed by leaving the brows neutral, raising the lower eyelids, and shaping a distinctive mouth with the corners drawn back and up, lips parted, exposing the teeth.

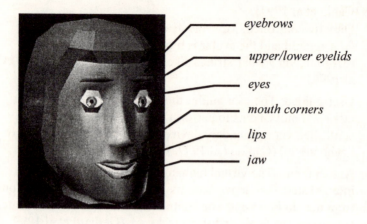

eyebrows

upper/lower eyelids

eyes

mouth corners

lips

jaw

Figure 7 Virtual head animation parameters

Experimental Work

We are currently undertaking controlled experiments to support our argument that emotionally expressive embodiments of students and teachers in VLEs can support, and enrich, the learning process for distant learners. We are comparing different approaches to the visualisation of inhabitants' emotional states in collaborative virtual environments. Preliminary findings in this ongoing research suggest that the psychological basis for recognising emotions can quite reasonably be applied to avatar-based interaction in VLE systems. The virtual interlocutor, depicting merely a few distinctive facial or physical clues, potentially takes on a personal and social role in the virtual space. It becomes a true representation of the underlying individual, not only visually, but also in a social and emotional context.

Furthermore, we will explore opportunities to make these embodiments autonomous to a certain degree, thereby creating permanent proxies for interaction and collaboration in the virtual learning space. The aim is to establish whether and how the social role the avatar potentially takes on when controlled by the underlying user can be maintained in absence of the user, and to investigate the benefits of this continuous virtual presence for the learning process.

However, strong evidence for the usefulness of user embodiments within educational CVEs can be found only by conducting large-scale empirical evaluation studies. CyberAxis is a project that potentially enables empirical evaluation of our research ideas, in order to further illuminate the crucial issue of establishing presence in VLEs.

CyberAxis

The Virtual Learning Environments Research Group at Leeds Metropolitan University in co-operation with Axis, an organisation for information on contemporary visual artists in Britain, are developing a Web-based, multi-user, virtual gallery. This joint project named *CyberAxis* is a Millenium Commission Lottery Project forming part of the Millennium Festival. The aim of the project is to increase the accessibility of contemporary British art by developing a public discussion forum for the Axis database.

The Axis database has been established as the National Artist Register since 1994, containing multimedia information on over 3,000 artists and 10,000 artworks. Full access to the Axis database is possible through the World Wide Web (http://www.axisartists.org.uk), from public *Axispoints* at various locations UK-wide, and at British Council offices around the globe. However, all current delivery routes of the Axis database have a traditional two-dimensional, multimedia, single-user interface.

Within the virtual gallery, avatars will represent visitors as well as artists. Avatars of artists will permanently inhabit this shared space, and means of verbal and non-verbal communication will be available to encourage the exchange of information and views on visual art between artists and visitors. The collection of data for the evaluation of the usability of the entire system in general, and our research ideas in particular, will be a special focus of the CyberAxis project.

Acknowledgements

CyberAxis is a Millenium Commission Lottery Project forming part of the Millennium Festival. The authors would like to thank Dennis McKenzie for the design of the virtual head Copyright virtual head geometry and processes Geometrek (www.geometrek.com).

References

Argyle, M. (1988) *Bodily Communication (second edition)*, New York, Methuen & Co. Inc.

Argyle, M. (1994) *The Psychology of Interpersonal Behaviour (Fifth edition)*, London, Penguin Books.

Bassili, J.N. (1978) Facial motion in the perception of faces and of emotional expressions, in *Journal of Experimental Psychology: Human Perception and Performance*, 4, 373-379.

Bates, A. W. (1998) Developing Networked Lifelong Learning Courses for Different Markets, in *Proceedings of Networked Lifelong Learning – Innovative Approaches to Education & Training Through the Internet*, International Conference, April 1998, University of Sheffield, UK, ISBN 1 899 323 05 1.

Benford, S.D., Bowers, J., Fahlén, L.E., Greenhalgh, C.M., Snowdon, D. (1995) User Embodiment in Collaborative Virtual Environments, in *Proceedings of 1995 ACM Conference on Human Factors in Computing Systems (CHI 95)*, Denver/Colorado, ACM Press.

Blaxxun (1999) Blaxxun ColonyCity homepage, URL *http://www.colonycity.com*

Bricken, M., Byrne, C. (1993) Summer Students in VR: A Pilot Study on Educational Applications in VR Technology, in *VR Application and Explorations*, Wexelblatt, A. (Ed.) Academic Press, Toronto, Canada.

Capin, T.K., Pandzic, I.S., Thalmann, N.M., Thalmann, D. (1997) Realistic Avatars and Autonomous Virtual Humans in VLNET Networked Virtual Environments, in *Virtual Worlds in the Internet*, Earnshaw, R.A., Vince, J. (eds.), IEEE Computer Society Press.

Carr, K. (1995) *Simulated and Virtual Realities: Elements of Perception*, Karen Carr and Rupert England (eds.), London, Taylor & Francis.

Dittrich, W.H. (1993) Action categories and the perception of biological motion, in *Perception*, 1993, 22, 15-22.

Dittrich, W.H., Troscianko, T., Lea, S.E.G., Morgan, D. (1996) Perception of emotion from dynamic point-light displays presented in dance, in *Perception*, 25, 727-738.

Ekman, P., Friesen, W.F. (1978) *Facial Action Coding* System, Consulting Psychologists Press Inc.

Ellis, S. R. (1995) Virtual Environments and Environmental Instruments, in *Simulated and Virtual Realities: Elements of Perception*, Karen Carr and Rupert England (eds.), London, Taylor & Francis, 11-51.

Fabri, M. (1998) Collaborative Virtual Environments as a Communication Tool for Distance Learning, in *Proceedings of Networked Lifelong Learning – Innovative Approaches to Education & Training Through the Internet*, International Conference, April 1998, University of Sheffield, UK, ISBN 1 899 323 05 1.

Fabri, M., Gerhard, M., Moore, D.J., Hobbs, D.J. (1999) Perceiving the Others: Cognitive Processes in Collaborative Virtual Environments, in *Proceedings of 17th Annual Conference of the Eurographics-UK Chapter*, April 1999, Cambridge, UK .

Fabri, M., Hobbs, D.J. (1998) What you see is what I mean: Virtual Encounters in Distance Learning Systems, in *Proceedings of 4th International Conference on Network Entities - Networking for the Millennium (NETIES 98)*, October 1998, Leeds, UK.

Franklin, S., Graesser, A. (1996) A Taxonomy for Autonomous Agents, in *Proceedings of the 3rd International Workshop on Agent Theories, Architectures, and Languages*, Springer, Berlin, Germany.

Garrison, R. (1993) Quality and access in distance education: theoretical considerations, in *Theoretical Principles of Distance Education*, Desmond Keegan (Ed.), New York, Routledge, 9-21.

Gerhard, M. (1997) A Hybrid Avatar/Agent Model for the Representation of Users within CVE's, in *Proceedings of Human Computer Interaction 1997 (HCI 97) (companion)*, Bristol, UK.

Gerhard, M., Fabri, M., Moore, D.J., Hobbs, D.J. (1999) Agents for Networked Virtual Learning Environments, in *Proceedings of 5th International Conference on Network Entities (NETIES 99)*, March 1999, Krems, Austria.

Gerhard, M., Moore, D.J. (1998) User Representation in Educational CVEs: Towards Continuous Presence, in *Proceedings of Network Entities 1998 - Networking for the Millennium (NETIES 98)*, October 1998, Leeds, UK.

Gibbs, G., Henry, M. (1996) coMentor, A Visual MUD System on the WWW, in Proceedings of Collaborative Virtual Environments 1996 (CVE 96), Nottingham, UK.

Godenschweger, F., Strothotte, T., Wagener, H. (1997) Rendering Gestures as Line Drawings, in Proceedings of International Gesture Workshop 1997 (GW97), Bielefeld, Germany, September 1997, Springer Verlag, ISBN 3 540 64424 5.

Hobbs, D.J., Taylor, R.J. (1998) Distance Learning across the Internet – An Examination of the Potential of Electronic Networking to Provide Effective Virtual Educational Environments, in *Proceedings of 4th International Conference on Network Entities - Networking for the Millennium (NETIES 98)*, October 1998, Leeds, UK.

Huxor, A. (1998) The Role of 3D Shared Worlds in Support of Chance Encounters in CSCW, in *Proceedings of International Conference on Digital Convergence: The Future of the Internet & WWW*, April 1998, Bradford, UK.

Johnson, W.L., Rickel, J., Stiles, R., & Munro, A. (1998) Integrating Pedagogical Agents into Virtual Environments, in *Presence: Teleoperators and Virtual Environments*, 7(6), MIT Press.

Knapp, M.L. (1978) *Nonverbal Communication in Human Interaction (2*nd Edition) Holt, Rinehart and Winston Inc., New York.

Laurillard, D. (1993) *Rethinking University Teaching, A Framework for the Effective Use of Educational Technology*, London, Routledge.

Laurillard, D. (1995) Multimedia and the Changing Experience of the Learner, *in British Journal of Educational Technology*, Vol. 26 No. 3, 179-189.

Loomis, J.M. (1992) Distal Attribution and Presence, in *Presence: Teleoperators and Virtual Environments*, Vol. 1, MIT Press, Boston, USA.

Maes, P. (1995) Artificial Life Meets Entertainment: Life like Autonomous Agents, in *Communications of the ACM*, 1995, USA.

Maes, P. (1997) in "The Future of Software Agents", in Roundtable Iconline, Institute of Electrical Engineers, USA. [http://computer.org/internet.v1n4/round2.htm].

Mann, J., Mon-Williams, M. (1996) What does Virtual Reality Need?: human factors issues in the design of 3D computer environments, in *International Journal of Human-Computer Studies,* Vol. 44, No 6, USA.

McShea, J., Jennings, S., McShea, H. (1997) Characterising User Control of Video Conferencing in Distance Education, in *Proceedings of CAL-97*, Exeter University.

Mitchell, W.L. (1997) Moving the museum onto the Internet: The use of virtual environments in education about ancient Egypt, in *Proceedings of From Desk-Top to Web-Top: Virtual Environments on the Internet, WWW & Networks,* International Conference, April 1997, Bradford, UK.

Moore, M.G. (1993) Three Types of Interaction, in *Distance Education: New Perspectives*, Keith Harry, Magnus John and Desmond Keegan (eds.), London, Routledge.

Morris, D., Collett, P., Marsh, P., O'Shaughnessy, M. (1979) *Gestures, their Origin and Distribution*, London, Jonathan Cape Ltd.

Neisser, U. (1976) *Cognition and Reality*, San Francisco, Freeman.

O'Malley, C. (1995) *Computer Supported Collaborative Learning*, Springer Press, Berlin, Germany.

Ødegård, O. (1993) Telecommunications and Social Interaction: social construction of virtual space, in *Telektronikk*, No. 4, W. H. Lie (Ed.), 128ff.

Pandzic, I.S., Kalra, P., Magnenat-Thalmann N., Thalmann D. (1994) Real-Time Facial Interaction, in *Displays*, 15(3).

Psotka, J., (1995), Immersive Tutoring Systems: Virtual Reality and Education and Training, in *Instructional Science*, Vol. 23, USA.

Roehl, B. (1998), Modelling and Animation of Virtual Humans, in Proceedings of Computer Vision for Virtual Human Modelling, IEEE Colloquium 1998/433, July 1998, London.

Rosenblum, L. (1997) Applications of the Responsive Workbench, in *IEEE Computer Graphics and Applications*, 17 (4), July-August 1997, 10-15 .

Rowntree, D. (1993) Exploring Open and Distance Learning, London, Kogan Page

Slater, M., Usoh, M. (1994) Body Centred Interaction in Immersive Virtual Environments, in *Artificial Life and Virtual Reality*, Nadia M. Thalmann and Daniel Thalmann (eds.), John Wiley & Sons, 125-148.

Slater, M., Wilbur S. (1997) A Framework for Immersive Virtual Environments (FIVE): Speculations on the Role of Presence in Virtual Environments, in *Presence: Teleoperators and Virtual Environments*, 6 (6), 603-616, MIT Press.

Slater, M., Steed, A., McCarthy, J., Maringelli, F. (1998) The Influence of Body Movement on Subjective Presence in Virtual Environment, in *Human Factors: The Journal of the Human Factors and Ergonomics Society* (in press).

Stoney, S., Wild, M. (1998) Motivation and interface design: maximising learning opportunities, in *Journal of Computer Assisted Learning*, 14, 40-50, Blackwell Science Ltd.

Tromp, J.G. (1995) Presence, Tele-Presence and Immersion: The Cognitive Factors of Embodiment and Interaction in Virtual Environments, in *Proceedings of Framework for Immersive Virtual Environments (FIVE 95)*, December 1995, London.

Wilson, T., Whitelock, D. (1998) CMC and how it transforms study by distance learners, in *Proceedings of Network Entities 1998 - Networking for the Millennium (NETIES 98)*, October 1998, Leeds, UK.

Witmer, B.G., Singer, M.J. (1998) Measuring Presence in Virtual Environments: a Presence Questionnaire, in *Presence: Teleoperators and Virtual Environments*, 7(3) June 1998, 225-240, MIT Press.

Zebrowitz, L.A. (1997) *Reading Faces: Window to the Soul?*, Boulder, Colorado, Westview Press.

4 Supporting Flexible Learning over the Net

LYNNE HALL, ADRIAN GORDON AND PAUL BLACK
UNIVERSITY OF NORTHUMBRIA AT NEWCASTLE, UK

Abstract

Students entering Higher Education now do so at a wide variety of ages and with different personal experiences. This increased accessibility to HE has resulted in an awareness that learning does not need to follow some predetermined path and that learning can indeed be a lifelong experience, not simply restricted to early adulthood.

HE institutions need to determine how best to serve this new demand. The willingness to accommodate the changing student population can be seen in the increased number of modes within which a student can study: full-time, part-time and by distance learning. However, lifelong learning demands a flexible mode of delivery that spans all of these. Although distance learning has had considerable success, many students fail to complete courses. A key factor in this is the sense of isolation amongst distance learners and a perceived lack of support.

Internet technologies offer a new range of opportunities to educators for the teaching and learning process. In this chapter we discuss one approach, using the VALIENT environment, which is being built specifically to support flexible and distance learning. This environment aims to offer the maximum flexibility to learners whilst maintaining a degree of support and interaction that will reduce the sense of isolation and alleviate the problems of studying primarily alone.

Introduction

The past decade has seen considerable changes in Higher Education, as the numbers of students studying for degree and Higher National courses has steadily increased, and government policy indicates that this trend towards mass education will continue. Nor has this increase in numbers focussed solely on the school/college input, rather HE has now become of interest to many sectors of the adult population. Students entering Higher Education now do so at a wide variety of ages and with different personal experiences. Rather than the 20-year-old direct entrant living on campus with few family responsibilities, there is a growing requirement to support mature students who may study in a part time or distance-learning mode (Jelly, 1997).

This increased accessibility to HE has resulted in awareness that learning does not need to follow some predetermined path and that learning can indeed be a lifelong experience, not simply restricted to early adulthood. The Dearing Report (Dearing, 1997): "Higher Education in the Learning Society" provides a strong focus on the need for life long learning and details a number of recommendations in relation to this. Amongst these recommendations, the report states, "We recommend to the Government and the Funding Bodies that, when allocating funds for the expansion of higher education, they give priority to those institutions which can demonstrate a commitment to widening participation". This recommendation encourages HE institutions to focus on serving sectors of the population possibly in different ways to those currently used.

Life long learning forces us to contemplate how best to serve a range of learners who may have very different needs to those who enter directly from schools and colleges. This form of learning also presupposes that many learners will be in employment and their study will not occur within traditional hours. However, further than this, lifelong learning assumes that learners will be home-based, in direct parallel to the steadily increasing numbers of homeworkers.

Distance learning

Learners who are unable to attend site-based courses have been served for many years through the distance-learning mode, and this provides one of the major delivery mechanisms for education. In 1989 (Mason & Kaye, 1989), there were over ten million distance learners and this number has steadily increased. Distance learning now involves a range of different media with which to enable students to learn, including paper, video, audio, computer based learning packages, etc. However, a key issue with such media is that it is non-interactive, where interaction is taken to be an activity shared with at least one other person.

Many distance-learning courses provide some interaction between the various learners participating in the course. Many hold seminars or summer schools and yearlong support and interaction with the HE institution and its staff is often provided using phone or letter/email, etc. However, most of the time, distance learners are working in isolation, often with virtually no interaction with any other person involved in the distance learning process (whether this be staff or fellow students).

The high wastage rates of distance learning (ICDE, 1998) can be at least partially explained by the sense of isolation felt by distance learners. This can have severe, negative effects on motivation, enthusiasm and interest in the subject material. Further, this isolation can mean an inability for some distance learners to progress in their learning due to problems in understanding the material. In a site-based environment, most students can ask their colleagues for advice and ideas. Simply discussing a task may help to expand a student's knowledge and understanding of an issue. For the majority of distance learners solitude is more the norm than group discussions.

ICTs as a delivery channel for distance learning

The model of distance learning, where materials are predominantly delivered via the postal service, and students meet once a year, is changing due to the improvements in Information and Communications Technologies (ICTs). It has been noted that ICTs can offer considerable possibilities in enhancing the learning experience of distance learners (Turoff, 1990). To ensure that ICTs do perform this function, considerable care is needed in both the design and deployment of ICT based learning provision. Such technologies (particularly those related to the use of the Internet) do offer a new range of opportunities to educators for the teaching and learning process. However, the use of a new delivery channel provokes a vast range of requirements and issues that need to be dealt with prior to its successful incorporation into Distance Learning.

Although there are many philosophical, social and educational implications of this move away from site-based study, distance learning, or as it is now being termed flexible and distance learning will emerge as a key delivery mechanism in the next century. This supposition can be based on a number of points:

– Government policy to increase participation in education for all sectors of the adult population.

– Funding needs of Higher Education Institutions, with many institutions seeking to increase their revenues due to the lack of public funding. In addition, flexible and distance learning is seen by HE management, as being a cost effective way of teaching and learning, although this can be related to the misunderstanding by some non-academic faculty of the true cost of providing distance learning (Bates, 1995).

- Increasing changes in needed skills within the workforce. This results in mature students seeking to enter the educational process an attempt to change career or to open up new avenues. Dearing's proposed multi-level sub-degree structure appears to be aimed at this type of student.

- The Learning Organisation is a concept that has been embraced by many companies. The focus on continuing professional development (often funded) means that employees may willingly undertake courses of study in relation to their work. In some organisations this can be obligatory; examples include the C.Eng. of the IEE (in some engineering companies).

- Major investments by Educational Institutions. Most UK universities are dedicating some resource to flexible and distance learning using ICT's both as a way in which to increase student numbers whilst only minimally increasing resources (a criticism of distance learning initiatives) and as a means of developing some kind of competitive advantage in the sector.

Learning Environment Requirements for Distance Learners

The awareness that flexible and distance learning is becoming an important distribution channel for education necessitates some consideration of the requirements that would be placed upon any such channel. The aim with distance learning is to provide an environment that facilitates flexible, independent, self-paced learning. Further, this environment must provide a highly usable forum where the learning focuses on the assimilation of the content, not the learning of the software application that enables access to the content. In our experience we would suggest that an environment that intends to enable such learning will need to meet the following requirements:

Provision of declarative and procedural knowledge Within the majority of courses taught at the HE level, students need to assimilate both declarative and procedural knowledge. In an on-site situation, declarative knowledge is usually provided in instructional blocks in the form of lectures, and is learning "by being told". Procedural knowledge is obtained through practical application and in the on-site mode occurs in the format of seminars, tutorials and lab classes; and is learning "by doing".

In a distance-learning environment, it is essential to provide facilities that enable and encourage learners to gain both types of knowledge in order to achieve a thorough understanding of the subject being studied. This means that both instructional and experiential learning experiences need to be provided. The former is less problematic, due to the fact that current distance learning makes wide use of instructional material in the form of books and lecture notes. This is relatively easy to convert into an electronic format.

Experiential learning is more problematic, bringing with it a variety of issues, primarily related to the fact that in an on-site situation, high quality interaction with an educator is guaranteed, and the educator can ensure the learner's comprehension of procedural knowledge. The requirement of an environment to support distance learning is to provide a supportive forum for practising activities traditionally learned in a classroom environment. Issues that need to be considered include the need to provide early, appropriate and continuous feedback to the learner about the quality of their solution to a problem whilst they are attempting that problem.

Identification of a clear linkage between declarative and procedural knowledge Within an on-site situation there is a clear linkage between declarative and procedural knowledge, and the sequence of knowledge acquisition frequently emphasises the relationship between the two, so that learners can see the connection between them. Typical course structures have lectures that are supported by additional classroom activities, such as seminars or lab classes, and educators can identify the relationship between declarative and procedural knowledge. A primary requirement of a learning environment is to permit the reinforcement of methodological and theoretical models within an experiential setting and the understanding of practical techniques and methods within an instructional setting. This places a requirement on a distance-learning environment to provide an integrated approach to teaching and learning.

However, this integrated approach must be designed with the recognition that not all learners need exposure to the same information at the same time. There is an awareness of the need for information to be adaptively presented to individual learners meeting their learning needs and requirements (Brusilovsky, 1998) and this has been a key aim for VALIENT, namely to enable customised learning to occur.

Combating feelings of isolation of the distance learner A key issue to be addressed is the feeling of isolation that distance learners feel. It is essential to provide a supportive interactive environment, where learners are able to easily air their problems and obtain solutions either from staff or other learners. Further, it is beneficial to provide of an environment in which collaborative learning can occur without the restriction of geographical proximity, and which can reduce the feeling of the learner that they are alone in the learning experience.

These requirements have emerged from our experience in developing flexible and distance learning material for a range of computing courses. It can be suggested that such requirements would be equally applicable for a variety of engineering style disciplines where there is a focus on experiential as well as theoretical learning. To illustrate our general approach to flexible and distance learning, we will be using the domain of database design as an example, as this is the area in which we have most experience and within which we have most fully developed our approach.

The Learning Environment

In the following sections of this article, we will describe the database design domain, identifying areas of that domain, which are problematical from the perspective of flexible and distance learning. Some of those areas of difficulty are specific to the database design domain, but many are of general significance. These include the integration of declarative and procedural knowledge in a coherent manner; the provision of appropriate and timely feedback in experiential task performance; the adaptation of pedagogical support to individual students; and the amelioration of the problems caused by feelings of isolation on the part of the distance learner.

Having considered the domain and its inherent difficulties, we will then describe our approach to addressing these, through the support of a number of separate pedagogical learning strategies. However, the true benefit of our approach lies in the integration of these pedagogical learning strategies into a single computational architecture. This architecture, VALIENT, is discussed in the final section.

Database design

Database design is taught in almost all undergraduate computing and IT courses (McLeod, 1996) and is widely used within software development in industry. In the following sections we focus on our attempts to support one aspect of database design, that of Entity Relationship (ER) modelling (Chen, 1976), (Teorey et al, 1986). This is a fundamental technique of database design, used to capture the data requirements of an information system, in terms of Entities, "things about which we wish to store data" and the Relationships between these Entities.

In a typical undergraduate course in ER modelling the subject is introduced via a series of lectures that provide the conceptual background to the problem, introduce notation and describe the procedural and analytical techniques used to build ER models. Armed with this basically declarative knowledge, learners must then gain extensive practical experience at solving ER modelling problems before they can be considered to be competent ER modellers. Typically this experience is gained by undertaking a set of pencil and paper exercises, either individually or in small groups, based around pre-prepared text based scenarios which must be analysed to produce data requirements which will be expressed as ER models.

The key point here is that extensive tutorial support is essential in the early stages of this learning process. Although ER models have intuitively simple constructs (Batra et al, 1990), novices find ER modelling difficult and exhibit systematic errors in their models (Hall & Gordon, 1998). Learners do not experience problems in using the notation (i.e. physically drawing the model); instead, errors are mostly made in relation to the application of an appropriate methodology (Hoggarth & Lockyer, 1996). The problems of ER modelling are compounded by a widely observed anchoring heuristic (Batra & Antony, 1994), whereby learners become reluctant to review any parts of a model that they have already constructed. Frequently, learners anchor to an incorrect model. Without appropriate and timely feedback from an educator, a learner will not be aware that they have constructed an incorrect model.

It is clear that this domain requires the provision of both declarative and procedural knowledge strongly integrated with experiential learning activities. Further, it is essential that tutorial support be tailored for individual learner's needs. The domain also shares the problems that are inherent for distance learners of any discipline, namely the perception of isolation, since in the classroom learners seem to naturally gravitate towards working in small groups to solve ER modelling problems. The next sections describe how we address each of these problems. To deliver the declarative and procedural knowledge to the learner a conventional website is used. To offer extensive experiential learning opportunities we have built several virtual learning environments. To provide support to the learner we use a combination of interactive on-line seminars and a bulletin board system.

Web-based instruction

Declarative and procedural knowledge about the database design domain is delivered via the World Wide Web. The material delivered in this way was developed through the conversion of already existing database design teaching materials. This use of existing material is fairly typical of on-line delivery of distance learning material and a number of different examples can be cited (Brennecke & Keil-Slawik, 1995), (Nichols, 1996).

Within our website, the material is structured as web pages: whereby the user is taken through a number of different themes as they follow through the structure of the web. This website includes text, graphics, animations, applets with worked examples and so on. Basically, this website contains lecture slides and accompanying notes, practical exercises and their model solutions, past examination questions and model answers, etc.

This site shows a fairly conventional use of the web to provide information to learners, which can be seen on a variety of different websites from many learning institutions. Although some interactivity with the learner is achieved through the use of forms to provide multiple choice style questions and answers, the web is largely passive and uniform for all users. However, we recognise that the web has greater utility and functionality than simple homogeneous information provision, and our attempts to provide an adaptive web (that provides a tailored web for each individual student) are described later in the article.

Virtual learning environments (VLEs)

Our VLEs are based on the paradigm of Text Based Virtual Reality. Although originally used primarily for recreation (e.g. Chatrooms (Hammond, 1997) and Multi User Dimensions (Curtis, 1992)), such environments have recently begun to attract increasing attention from educators (Fanderclai, 1995). In this style of VLE, the virtual space is realised as a collection of locations or "rooms" connected to one another through the use of exits / doors in a virtual space. The educational opportunities afforded by such environments are based on the navigation around the virtual environment by the learner(s), and their manipulation of the objects found in that environment.

This leads to a move away from an instructivist pedagogical approach (such as computer-based tutorials) to what (Reeves, 1996) refers to as a constructivist approach. Of particular importance in such environments are the communication possibilities that they provide. Collaborating learners can communicate with one another synchronously while performing learning tasks.

Experiential tasks related to ER modelling are performed within an environment called ERM-VLE (Entity Relationship Modelling - Virtual Learning Environment) (Hall & Gordon, 1998). This provides the learner with a textual scenario that is distributed around the virtual space of ERM-VLE. In order to construct a model, the learner must navigate around in this virtual space, collecting and manipulating objects as she goes. The virtual space in ERM-VLE is made up of a number of interconnected locations of different types. Scenario rooms are locations where the learner can collect textual elements of the scenario. Other rooms represent locations where model elements can be built from elements of the scenario, such as Entity Creation rooms, and Relationship Creation rooms.

The task structure of the ER modelling problem is reflected in the topological organisation of the virtual world. For example, learners are not allowed to progress beyond the Entity Creation rooms before all entities from the scenario have been correctly identified. By implicitly embodying a method for ER modelling in the virtual world, learners are encouraged to follow an ordered rather than a chaotic task sequence (as is often observed in novice learners).

As well as being encouraged to follow a structured task sequence, learners are given immediate feedback about the correctness of their model as they are building it (thus counteracting the anchoring heuristic). This feedback is provided by intelligent pedagogical agents. These agents basically perform the role of the tutor, providing feedback about the quality of a learner's solution to a problem while that problem is being attempted. Such agents have been used with some success in a number of applications. For example, in MEMOLAB (Dillenbourg et al, 1994) teaching agents (which due to their teaching style are considered to be either tutors or coaches) provide support for learners in the acquisition of basic methodological skills in experimental psychology. In the GRACILE project (Ayala & Sano, 1994), a number of different agents exist to aid students in learning Japanese. The agents within GRACILE are of different types: mediator agents act as facilitators, supporting communication and collaboration among learners; and domain agents have knowledge about sentence construction and language usage.

In ERM-VLE the pedagogical agents have access to a model solution for each scenario, and know about the correct correspondences between elements from the scenario and elements from the correct ER model for that scenario. They also have knowledge about the common errors that learners make when building ER models. Whenever learners attempt to build an incorrect part of an ER model, the pedagogical agent will intervene, and explain why the action that the learner is attempting is incorrect.

Supporting the learner

In an attempt to reduce the feelings of isolation of the student and to encourage peer learning, two supportive fora are provided. Firstly, a seminar forum is provided which learners can attend to interact both with one another and with the lecturer. This enables learners to discuss problems and issues relating to the subject material. This interactive seminar, (following the model of the Diversity University (Acker, 1995)) will occur at specified times. However, it is unlikely that all learners will always be able to (virtually) attend a particular seminar session. Thus, rather than the seminar being a one-off event, the tutor holding the seminar will identify key topics and provide mini-tutorials on these through the use of specially tailored Frequently Asked Question (FAQ) pages. Through linking these FAQs to form-based tests and to specific scenarios within the VLEs, "revision" of these topics is made possible.

A second level of support is provided through the use of bulletin boards. These are similar to news or user groups developed within a web context. They provide a means for users to obtain information and additionally to post questions that other users of the boards may respond to. It has been identified that bulletin boards can result in empathic communities (Preece, 1998), where the various users of these boards provide empathic support to one another. This potential for empathy and for a sense of belonging as reported by Preece, suggests the suitability of bulletin boards as a support mechanism for distance learners, providing them with a communication forum with others who are in a similar situation to themselves.

The bulletin board enables learners to post queries relating to aspects of the course that they do not fully understand. Although a staff member monitors these boards, the aim of their use is for other learners to respond to their peers. This can provoke discussion, albeit asynchronous, and also helps to develop a feeling of community amongst separate learners.

VALIENT

Each of the net-based facilities previously discussed is integrated into an architecture called VALIENT (Virtual Autonomous Learning Integrated Environment using Net-based Technologies). All of these facilities can be accessed by the learner using a conventional web browser. Using this browser, learners can access the web-based learning material, they can start up and interact with the Virtual Learning Environments (such as ERM-VLE), and they can use the bulletin board, attend virtual seminars, use FAQs, send emails to their tutors and other colleagues, etc.

We believe that the true benefits of the VALIENT environment lie in the *integration* of different learning styles embodied in these diverse facilities, which have been provided through the use of a variety of net-based technologies. The most striking example of the benefits of this integration can be seen in the way that tutorial support can be tailored to the needs of the individual learner by exploiting the knowledge of the pedagogical agents that are to be found in VALIENT's Virtual Learning Environments. By doing so we have been able to achieve what is effectively an adaptive educational website.

VALIENT's adaptive web

Current educational uses of the web have largely failed to benefit from the web's flexibility, and the real potential of the web is being underused. The main strength of the web is in providing information. However, not all learners require the same information, nor do they require it in the same order. (Brusilovsky, 1998) discusses the emergence of "adaptive presentation technologies" in which information can be dynamically generated, and individually tailored to the goals and current level of knowledge of each learner.

VALIENT achieves this information tailoring by communicating with the pedagogical agents that are to be found in the database design intelligent learning environments, such as ERM-VLE. These pedagogical agents are able to diagnose student misconceptions about the database design process. However, as well as providing feedback to the student, they inform VALIENT about their diagnosis. On the basis of this diagnosis, VALIENT can then choose appropriate resources that are to be presented to the learner, such as detailed explanations, appropriate illustrative examples, model solutions, simpler exercises etc.

VALIENT is based around an intelligent web server system (implemented as a servlet in Java) that replaces the functionality of conventional web servers and coordinates the presentation of learning material to a learner. This extension of the web and its integration with other net based technologies signals a move away from the passive learning approach of earlier technologies towards a more interactive, constructive, communicative learning experience that forms the basis of a true on-line learning community.

Discussion

The various components of VALIENT are nearing completion and we are now in the process of integrating this environment to begin evaluation with students in the winter semester of 1998. Through evaluating this environment with learners in our full and part time modes we aim to gain the maximum information possible to adapt this environment to the needs of learners who will be distant from the university. VALIENT provides an architecture that enables students to benefit from both experiential and content-based instruction, with knowledge provided at both the procedural and declarative level. Rather than being faced with pages of web-based material and having to sift through these to gain the appropriate knowledge, students will be presented with manageable, customised chunks of information focused on their needs. By constantly monitoring students within VALIENT, we can identify those who have particular difficulties, and respond appropriately.

Our own work and that of previous researchers has clearly indicated that each of the component technologies that make up VALIENT are useful in their own right. However, we believe that the synergy resulting from the integration of these technologies will provide learners with a much richer learning experience.

Although VALIENT is being tested in the domain of database design, it appears that it will be useful across a number of different domains. VALIENT is itself domain independent and provides a framework within which to base the learning experience. We believe that this environment will have considerable utility and will provide a new and effective way for students to learn.

References

Acker S.R. (1995); Space, collaboration, and the credible city: Academic work in the virtual university, *Journal of Computer-Mediated Communication*, 1 (1).

Ayala G. and Yano Y. (1994); Design Issues in a Collaborative Intelligent Learning Environment for Japanese Language Patterns, *Proc. ED-MEDIA 94*, AACE, Vancouver, Canada, 67-72.

Bates A.W. (1995); Technology: Open Learning and Distance Education, New York: Routledge.

Batra D. and Antony S.R. (1994); Novice errors in conceptual database design. *European journal of information systems* 3(1), 57-69.

Batra D. Hoffer. J A. Bostrom R P. (1990); Comparing Representations with Relational and ER Models, *Commun. ACM*, 33 (2), 126-139.

Brennecke A. and Keil-Slawik R. (1995); Notes on the "Alltagspraxis" of Hypermedia Design, in Maurer, H. (Ed), *Proceedings of IFIP-Conference ED-MEDIA 95 – World Conference on Educational Multimedia and Hypermedia, Charlottesville (VA) Association for the Advancement of Computing in Education*, 115-120.

Brusilovsky P. (1998); Adaptive Educational Systems on the World Wide Web. in *Proceedings of the World Congress on Expert Systems Workshop on Current Trends and Applications of Artificial Intelligence in Education*, 9-16.

Chen P.P. (1976); The entity-relationship model - towards a unified view of data. *ACM Transactions on Database systems* 1(1) 9-36.

Curtis P. (1992); Mudding: Social Phenomena in Text-Based Virtual Realities". *Xerox PARC technical report CSL-92-4*, available at. ftp://parcftp.xerox.com/pub/MOO/papers/DIAC92.txt.

Dearing R. (1997); Higher Education in the Learning Society, available at http://www.leeds.ac.uk/ncihe/index.htm.

Dillenbourg P. Mendelsohn P. Schneider D. (1994); The Distribution of Pedagogical Roles in a Multi-agent Learning Environment, in Lewis, R. & Mendelsohn, P. (Eds): *Lessons from Learning*, Amsterdam: North-Holland.

Fanderclai T.L. (1995); MUDs in Education: New Environments, New Pedagogues, *CMC Magazine*, 2 (1).

Hall L. and Gordon A. (1998); A Virtual Learning Environment for Entity Relationship Modelling, *ACM SIGCSE Conference 98*, Atlanta.

Hammond R, (1997); History of the Internet: *WWW, IRC, and MUDs*, available at http://www.socio.demon.co.uk/history.html.

Hannafin M J. (1992); Emerging technologies, ISD, and learning environments: Critical perspectives, *Educational Technology Research and Development*, 40 (1), 49-63.

Hoggarth G.R. and Lockyer M.A. (1996); Systems development methods guidance and CASE: integration between CASE and CAL, *Software Engineering Journal*, May, 141-147.

International Council for Distance Education (ICDE) homepage available at http://www.cde.psu.edu/ICDE/.

Jelly I. (1997); Whom are we teaching? *Computer* 30(11). 49-50.

Mason R. and Kaye A. (1989); *Mindweave: Communication, Computers and Distance Education*, Oxford, Pergamon.

McLeod R. (1996); Comparing undergraduate courses in systems analysis and design. *Communications of the ACM* 39(5), 113-121.

Nichols D.M. (1996); Educational Web Resources: is the Brussels metro useful?, in *1st CSALT Workshop on the Design of WWW Resources for Learning,* at http://www.comp.lancs.ac.uk/csalt/Workshop/dmntalk/.

Preece J. (1998); Empathic Communities: Reaching Out Across the Web, in *Interactions,* Vol. V2, 32-43.

Reeves T. (1996); Evaluating What Really Matters in Computer-Based Education, at http://www.oltc.edu.au/cp/refs/reeves.html

Teorey T.J., Yang D. and Fry J.P. (1986); A Logical Design Methodology for Relational Databases Using the Extended Entity-Relationship Model. *Computing Surveys*, 18 (12), 197-222.

Turoff M. (1990); *Foreword to On-Line Education: Perspectives on a New Environment*, Harasim, L., New York: Praeger Publishers.

5 The Potential of Electronic Networking to Provide Effective Learning Environments

DAVE HOBBS, RIK TAYLOR AND JAMES ARMSTRONG
LEEDS METROPOLITAN UNIVERSITY, UK

Abstract

Although interest in the WWW as a means to teach and to empower students is increasing, on-line classrooms are still few and far between. However, the newer Internet technologies may help change this. For example, developers are now experimenting with technologies that can provide users with reliable synchronous communication, using video cameras to provide access to live discussions in a WWW environment.

This chapter discusses the various technologies and the uses to which they have been put over the Internet. It then goes on to describe practical case studies - experimental work at LMU that has attempted to learn more about the application of these technologies. For example, one LMU project (Section 7) designed an intelligent support system for users as they attempt to navigate through hypermedia-based educational materials, the type of material which is becoming increasingly utilised by CD-ROM reference materials as well as being the format of the World Wide Web.

Another research project at LMU (Sections 8 and 9) involved designing, developing and evaluating a prototype WWW-based multimedia teaching tool - a test using HTML forms, colour images and MPEG video. The project was conducted between sites in the UK and Australia using the WWW and other Internet functionality to exchange and share information, giving valuable first-hand experience of the benefits and frustrations of on-line co-operative working.

A third LMU research project (Sections 10 and 11) took this further and studied the applicability of teleworking technology within educational environments in general and compared collaborative working using email with the process of working together on such tasks in a face-to-face situation. Of particular interest were the perceptions of the participants regarding the collaborative process, as well as the efficacy of the process itself in terms of its outcome.

Internet Functionality

The WWW has achieved enormous success largely through word of mouth coupled with the enthusiastic support of the media, and commercial interests have adopted the WWW as a new advertising and marketing medium. Along with this increase in popularity, there has been a rush to incorporate new features into the associated software, many of which can facilitate and enhance specific educational modes discussed later in this chapter. For example, as HTML has evolved, functionality has been added such as interactive forms, more versatile layout styles, and cascading style sheets. An interesting area is the integration of new Internet technologies into the WWW. For instance, Internet Relay Chats (real-time group discussions) and MUDs (Multiple User Dungeons - essentially an IRC in an interesting setting) provide users and designers with the ability to interact with each other live instead of, for example, having to wait for a mailing list to distribute the information as it is posted via email. Another Internet technology being integrated into the WWW is CUSeeMe sites (http://www.cuseeme.com). CUSeeMe is a teleconferencing program that allows multiple users to see and hear each other by converting the data from a video camera into an Internet compatible format. Functionality such as this combined with the WWW's built-in audio-visual capabilities suggests new possibilities for group-based on-line education.

Another major influence on the WWW in a major way is the rapidly increasing use of Java applets within HTML pages. The Java language is the first to present a comprehensive solution to the challenges of programming for the Internet, providing an object-oriented programming language optimised for the creation of distributed, executable applications and offering portability, security, advanced networking and reliability without compromising performance. Applications written in Java can migrate transparently over the Internet, accessible by anyone using a Java enabled web browser. Both Netscape Navigator and Microsoft Internet Explorer, the most popular WWW browsers, offer Java support enabling them to download Java applets to run on a wide variety of client systems. Java has been available since April 1995 for developers using the Sun Solaris or

SunOS platforms. More recently the availability of the language has been extended to other varieties of UNIX, Microsoft's Windows NT and Windows 95/98 operating systems.

The Real (http://www.realaudio.com/) player is another good example of how WWW technology is being advanced. This gives WWW users equipped with only a standard multimedia personal computer and a 56Kbps or faster modem instantaneous access to real-time audio and video streaming. It uses highly compressed media files that, rather than being downloaded and then played as a complete file, are received incrementally, buffered and then each segment fed to the Real player as it arrives, thus enabling continuous play from the outset. This technology makes audio-on-demand and video-on-demand as practical as delivery of text and graphics, overcoming the significant downloading delays that have hitherto presented an obstacle to its informational, recreational and creative use.

WWW browser 'plug-ins' are written by third parties and extend the functionality of the browser still further, offering features such as video and audio compression and decoding, virtual reality mark-up language (VRML) support, and video/audio conferencing within the browser's Graphical User Interface.

The WWW for Research and Information Seeking

The WWW has grown from its origins as a simple system for distributing documents and communicating among members of the high-energy physics community into a more general multimedia tool of wider appeal. Nevertheless, its use as a research tool continues and has increased enormously. Research institutions and universities have established home pages and the WWW is increasingly used to advertise the work and interests of departments and staff. Researchers are still some of the keenest users of the WWW in view of its potential for contact and collaboration, for disseminating research findings, and for facilitating peer review of the outcomes of research (Russell and Baird 1995).

Despite the magnitude of the information available, using the Web is a simple matter, even for young children, so that anyone with the desire and the time to explore is bound to discover a variety of fascinating sites and resources. Because of the vast numbers of WWW sites, knowing where to begin searching, what to look for, and what to ignore can be a daunting task. The development of what are known as webworms, spiders, and knowbots (computerised search agents which will scan the Internet looking for requested information) has facilitated the search process somewhat, although it has brought another problem in that an overwhelming amount of reference material may be returned. This has been helped somewhat by individual WWW users who have already begun to catalogue the enormous variety of educational resources available on-line. As this information is compiled, it becomes available to the educational community in the form of on-line resource guides, some of which are no more than hypertext lists of known educational resources.

The educational resources page created as part of a project conducted at LMU by Taylor (Hobbs and Taylor 1998) is an example of this kind of listing. A set of WWW pages (http://www.dstc.edu.au/~ taylor/education/) was developed to offer the reader a practical means of following up the educational resources discussed. The pages were designed and constructed featuring sites demonstrating interesting and innovative educational pages and existing on-line courses that were judged to exploit some of the best educational features of the WWW. As designers of WWW sites develop more on-line resource guides, the WWW will begin to resemble a World Wide Library Catalogue although, unlike a traditional library, the books and other documents that are available will have been created by students, lecturers and anyone else with an interest in contributing. In consequence, as the WWW grows, so will easy access to useful and interesting information. There are naturally concerns over the reliability of the knowledge that is being published on the WWW. Treloar (1995) suggests, however, that there is no reason why Web-published journals should not be subject to the same peer review processes that apply in the print world.

The WWW as Teaching Tool

From a curricular point of view, the WWW can be used to design tutorials and on-line lessons for a variety of subjects. For example, Blumberg (1994) describes an on-line teaching tool for basic genetics known as MendelWeb (http://www.netspace.org/MendelWeb/) that integrates elementary biology, discrete mathematics, and the history of science. MendelWeb is constructed from Gregor Mendel's 1865 paper *Experiments in Plant Hybridisation* presented as an active document, with links to traditional reference material (eg glossaries, biographies, and the original German text) as well as images, tutorials, active commentaries, related Web sites, and animations. Discussion and questions are presented as they would be in a live introduction to a biology course - students may choose in what order they wish to explore the topics, and thus they are able to develop their comprehension of the subject at their own rate.

The authors of such systems have usually carefully mapped out the possible outcomes of each piece of information offered. A successful WWW system such as MendelWeb will therefore be crafted with sometimes thousands of links and hundreds of pages. The proliferation of automatic HTML authoring programs suggests that creating such linkages in the future will no longer seem a daunting task. Furthermore, hyperbook design may become even further simplified through the use of intelligent computer programs which will analyse a document's content with inquisitive search agents in order to help formulate questions that might be raised by that content.

The WWW is therefore beginning to provide the necessary tools with which to design on-line teaching material. However the potential of WWW teaching packages has yet to be realised largely because most WWW books have been technically oriented. In order for this technology to reach the mainstream subject areas, WWW tutorials must be designed for less technical subjects like history, music, language, arts. For example, a site specialising in the complete works of Shakespeare site could include question and answer sessions, as well as audio and video clips of each play and poem. Using appropriate tools, the capability to transform a topic of choice into a document that could be useful and educational for students could be available to everyone.

Use of this type of educational hypermedia raises a number of user interface issues, a major one of which concerns user navigation - how on the one hand to prevent the user from becoming overwhelmed with information and losing track of their direction, whilst on the other hand permitting them to make the most of the facilities hypermedia offers. Two alternative approaches to this issue can be identified. One is initially to restrict the number of links made available to the student, and then dynamically to increase or reconfigure the available links as the user proceeds. The second approach is to make all the links available from the outset but seek to assist the user by one or more navigational aids. Through the research work of Mullier (1995a and 1995b) and Bell (1996) described in the Section 7 below, LMU has been exploring each of these approaches.

The WWW as Examiner

Another area which is very resource-intensive and which is therefore the target of many educational institutions seeking efficiency-savings in the current climate of financial cutbacks in educational funding is student assessment. Developments in HTML that introduced the ability of the

WWW to display fill-in forms can now also help create interactive educational pages, and educational sites have begun offering tests and quizzes for both assessment and self-assessment. The Podiatry test developed by Taylor (Hobbs and Taylor, 1998) and described in more detail in Section 8 below is an example of this kind of application on the WWW.

However, it is not yet sufficiently easy and productive for subject specialists to generate this kind of interactive software. For example, in the area of medicine that is very visually intense and information-rich (Cho 1994), it is difficult for medical practitioners with little training in computer science to write scripts that create and manage forms and interact with other software on the server. Another technical problem discussed by Ibrahim and Franklin (1995) in relation to these kinds of interactive applications is the fact that the http protocol is stateless in the sense that there is no direct relationship between two consecutive requests to the same server, even if the queries come from the same user. This means that the server treats every request it receives independently from any other request it received in the past or that it will receive in the future. From a technical perspective, this statelessness allows the http server software to impose very little overhead on the server machine, and keeps the protocol between the client and server very simple. Nevertheless, from a learning point of view the statelessness of the http protocol (meaning that the connection to a server is closed after a requested document is delivered) is a serious shortcoming preventing intelligent interaction. Fortunately ways around this are developing. For example, the use of 'cookies', small items of data sent to the user's computer, presents a mechanism for recording a session so that, having checked the state of the cookies at the start of a subsequent access of a site, the site's software can retrieve a memory of previous accesses and transactions.

The WWW as an Educational Forum

Proponents of the Internet have long promoted its use as a forum for discussion and as a marketplace for ideas and information. The WWW also fulfils this goal, and in terms of use in the education community, the WWW can provide a basis for virtual debate and discovery. All of the original uses of the Internet - including file transfer protocol (ftp), email, USENET news, and gopher continue to thrive in the context of the WWW and have now converged into a singular informational tool since the latest generation of WWW browsers, such as Netscape Navigator and the Microsoft Internet Explorer are capable of interacting with the full suite of Internet protocols.

Because of this, it is conceivable for a designer to utilise all of these services to set up a multimedia/hypermedia discussion on any given subject. As a basis for such discussions, Internet users have traditionally used mailing lists to form a discussion group, receiving information from and posting information to the mailing list via email, which in turn then distributes the information to everyone on the list. Recently, some organisations have even used mailing lists to run virtual conferences, where sometimes thousands of people sign up to an on-line discussion and take part in a week-long forum, all without leaving their homes or offices.

For educators, this combination of presentation (the WWW) and critique (mailing lists) can be used successfully in a variety of ways. For instance, a teacher could set up a WWW site that comprises the lectures, frequently asked questions, and multimedia presentations. Via a mailing list, students could automatically add information to that site in the form of additional questions, reports, essays, etc. In this case, they could use mail-to-HTML converters and so would not need to become experts in HTML. The software would then automatically append their message onto the page itself, so future site visitors will be able to read the comments. The educational potential of such a system cannot be ignored although the uncontrolled and unrefereed nature of the material again has to be borne in mind.

Students can also use the various Internet technologies to create their own hypertext work and then present it on-line so that their peers and lecturers may discuss and review it. Learning how to critique others' work and to present a persuasive, constructive argument are skills that are often gained slowly for many students, for they are rarely taught in any formal fashion (Laurillard 1995). Further, on-line electronic discussions apparently seem to be less threatening for some than standing up in front of peers. In addition, because conversation is electronic, it can be automatically catalogued and presented by the student as part of the project. This is not to propose that traditional class presentations should vanish with the advent of on-line class forums, but that allowing students to work with and learn from each other in such a way could encourage the many students who previously did not easily contribute voluntarily to a discussion.

The WWW in Collaborative Education

In its present form the WWW is not very well suited for collaborative work that requires a high degree of real-time interaction. Prototypes for synchronous communication such as Web-Chat exist but are currently unstable and slow. One of the most exciting recent developments for collaborative education are WWW interfaces to Multi-User Dungeons (MUDs) and Object-oriented MUDs (MOOs). Curtis and Nichols (1993) describe a MOO as a network-accessible, multi-user, programmable, interactive system well suited to the construction of text-based adventure games, conferencing systems, and other collaborative software. Its most common use, however, is as a multi-participant, low-bandwidth virtual reality. Participants give one-line commands that are parsed and interpreted as appropriate. Such commands may cause changes in the virtual reality, such as the location of a character, or may simply report on the current state of that reality, such as the appearance of some object. The database contains representations of all of the objects in the virtual reality, including the MOO programs that the server executes to give those objects their specific behaviours.

MOOs allow for individual users to extend the environment by 'building' or creating new objects. In an educational context this can allow the student to become an active participant in the learning experience. In addition, it is well documented in the literature that MOOs provide a strong sense of 'place', possibly bringing back some of the social intercourse of 'campus' life that is lost in distance education. A MOO server can also be configured to act as an http server. This means that a WWW browser can be used to look at locations, rooms, people, artefacts, etc. in the MOO. These objects can have hypertext URL's attached and therefore be used to structure information on the WWW. An example use of a MOO in an advanced educational setting is the Global Network Academy (GNA) 'Introduction to Object Orientated Programming using C++' course (http://info.desy.de/pub/uu-gna). The long-term goal of the GNA is to become a fully accredited on-line university. The course was built around four main components, a hyperbook, mailing lists, practical projects and MOO interactions (Perron 1994).

Case Study 1 - A Demonstration of the Educational Potential of the WWW for providing an intelligent support system for users navigating through hypermedia-based educational materials

Elsom-Cook (1989) has argued that the perfect tutoring system should be able to range between the two extremes of total constraint and total absence of constraint, in line with the student's current needs and state of knowledge. In a similar vein, Hartley (1993) proposes that when there is a mismatch between the strategy of the learning system and the learning style of the student, performance is degraded, suggesting a need to support different styles and viewpoints of users. With this in mind, one of Mullier's aims (Mullier 1995a and 1995b) was to build hypermedia systems with the ability to adapt to students' needs as they progress from novice to expert users, and ultimately to modify the pre-programmed strategy according to the students' experiences with other students. His current prototypes achieve this using a combination of knowledge-based representations ('semantic hypermedia') and neural network models ('connectionist modelling').

It is argued that this approach aims to overcome a major concern in the domain of educational hypermedia, namely the potential danger of the user becoming 'lost in hyperspace' and either not being presented with or else not managing to find the relevant information. The prototypes seek to deal with this concern by making more links available to users when their knowledge of the domain is judged to be improving. Through this mechanism they attempt to provide the graduated approach advocated by Elsom-Cook (1989) and thus to promote 'freedom without anarchy' - the novice user of the system being 'freed' by having much of the complexity associated with an unfamiliar system and subject hidden from him, while the more advanced student is 'freed' from constraints unhelpful to his level of mastery of the system.

A different, but not incompatible, approach from this adaptive hypermedia is to allow all users unrestricted access to all the system's links, but to seek to ameliorate the possible cognitive overhead using one or more navigational aids. Hutchings et al (1992) suggest that there are three categories of such devices *(direct access devices, history devices, and tours). Direct access devices* associate a unique object with each node in the system, either in the form of graphical objects or icons (maps and browsers), or keywords (contents and index lists), enabling users to 'jump' to any node in the system with one action. Examples of direct access devices are contents lists, maps, indexes, homing functions (Norman 1994) and landmarks (Nielsen 1993). *History devices* provide a record of nodes that have been viewed so that users may return to any previously visited node, or can recognise those nodes that have already been accessed. Examples of these are timestamp (Nielsen 1990), backtrack (Nielsen 1990), bookmarking and history list (Nielsen 1993). Finally, the use of *tours* seeks to remove the requirements for navigation by connecting a series of nodes together.

Despite this plethora of navigational aids, there is a relative lack of evidence to indicate how helpful these aids are to users of hypermedia systems in educational contexts. Bell (1996) therefore set up a series of experiments to cast some light on this issue. This involved designing and building hypermedia applications in areas being taught to LMU students, and assessing their efficacy when used by the students.

Overall the hypermedia system was well received, with problems of user disorientation lower than might have been expected. The hypothesised effectiveness of a local map was not, however, supported by the evidence. It may be that the additional aid provided a cognitive load that was not outweighed by its putative benefits, or else it could be that the local map was not implemented in the most effective manner. Alternatively, it might be that a slightly different map, or a similar map in a different domain, or else greater use of the current map in the current domain, would suggest a greater utility of the map than does the current evidence.

This indicates a case for more design and evaluation work of a similar nature. Ultimately, the aim of this research is to integrate its findings within on-going educational provision at LMU with a view to offering the students increasingly powerful student-based learning opportunities.

Case Study 2 - A Demonstration of the Educational Potential of the WWW through a Multimedia Based Teaching and Assessment Tool

The process of exploring the WWW is in itself an educational experience. There are however more structured ways that the WWW can be used in the educational context. With the continuing development of HTML and its ability to use display fill-in forms, courseware designers are now able to create educational material that has most of the characteristics of courseware built on stand-alone machines. To explore this capability further Taylor (Hobbs and Taylor 1998) developed and evaluated a WWW-based Podiatry test.

In consultation with a lecturer in the Podiatry School at Queensland University of Technology a Multimedia Podiatry Test (http://www.dstc.edu.au/~taylor/podiatry) was constructed on its home page. The questions for the test were taken from existing paper-based questions. Once completed, the test was demonstrated to a lecturer at the Podiatry School, and then to a practising podiatrist. The feedback from both parties was very encouraging. The lecturer considered that the functionality of the test would be a useful addition to the pedagogical tools available to him; the practising podiatrist was interested in the prospect of having available an on-line multimedia test incorporating high quality colour images and video since practising podiatrists in Australia are often spread over very large areas at considerable distance from a Podiatry School.

It is clear that multimedia has much to offer education. There is the potential for better quality courses, prepared by the best tutors. Furthermore, courses may be made consistent across and between organisations, and students generally seem to retain more from interactive multimedia training than traditional classroom courses. Equally important in the modern climate, cost reductions are made possible, as courses become available to more people, and it becomes increasingly feasible to cater for 'non-standard' students such as those wishing to study part-time or from work. There are, however, a number of potential drawbacks, one of which is the danger that the teaching interaction will become unduly didactic. As long ago as the mid 1980's, Girle (1986) expressed a concern that computer assisted learning systems might be based on assumptions about interactive communication that could put the style of interaction into a very narrow and inflexible mode. This is supported by Laurillard (1995) who believes that "too often the multimedia products on offer to education use the narrative mode, or unguided discovery, neither of which supports the learner well, nor exploits the capability of the medium". In a similar vein Moore and Hobbs (1997) identify limits to multimedia technology's capabilities in a training role, in particular with regard to individualised feedback and discussion. The danger is, therefore, that the multimedia teaching interaction becomes a one-way transfer of a body of reified knowledge, from the knowledgeable computer to the student lacking in that knowledge - the 'banking concept of education' (Friere 1972).

One possible approach to addressing this problem of untoward didacticism is to allow multiple participants in the learning interactions, so that learners are then able to use the environment to communicate, either synchronously or asynchronously, with each other and with their tutors through related developments such as the 'virtual school' eg Facemyer (1996), and the use of CSCDL - Computer Supported Collaborative Distributed Learning (Fjuk and Sorensen 1996). Skillcorn (1996) advocates a similar approach, seeing 'networked hypermedia courseware' as a possible solution to the economic demands on Higher Education and to student demand for flexible provision, and describing social interaction in hypermedia environments as yielding a 'community of learners'. Such an approach is clearly promising, but raises issues concerning control of the learners' use of the available resources (Nkambou and Gauthier 1996), network protocols (Trathern and Sajeev 1996), and communication protocols between users (Fjuk and Sorensen 1996).

The second approach is to have the computer itself be a participant in the learning interaction. For this to avoid the aforementioned danger of undue didacticism, the computer must be capable of engaging the student in suitable educational dialogue. This of course is a very complex endeavour (Baker 1994). Earlier research by Moore and Hobbs (1994) aimed to contribute to this endeavour by designing a system that would engage its student in educational debate on controversial issues such as capital punishment and abortion. This is seen as being important educationally in that debate can be expected to improve the student's critical faculties, helping him to adopt a questioning approach and to think for himself, rather than passively receiving input from his tutor or any other source (Moyse and Elsom-Cook 1992). This should result in a gain in awareness on the part of the student of the substantive points of dispute involved. The authors argue that scope for application is wide, for as Self (1992) points out: "... it is rarely possible to define a unique 'correct' viewpoint to be communicated to a student".

Case Study 3 - A Demonstration of the Educational Potential of the WWW for Distance Learning and Supervision

One obvious role for the WWW, using all of the above scenarios is in Distance Education (Ibrahim 1994). The United Kingdom's main distance educator, its largest University and also its largest publisher, namely the Open University (http://www.open.ac.uk), began several years ago to embrace and exploit the WWW. Compared to a traditional distance education system of paper and post, some of the benefits of the WWW for dissemination of material include the ability of the training centres to distribute the knowledge on a large scale almost instantaneously; the reduction of mailing costs which allows distribution of material without the overheads associated with printing and transport, the correction and updating of all information for all users from just one server site, the availability of a variety of different teaching styles and modes of communication between teachers and learners, facilitation of collaborative writing between authors, and improved mechanisms for students to give and receive feedback more easily.

Taylor's Podiatry project (described above in Section 8) was itself an exercise in distance education, as the research and practical work were completed in Australia with the supervisor based in the United Kingdom. All supervision of the project was performed over the Internet, with the majority of the communication using email. 'Interactive' progress meetings were conducted using the simple text based TALK program, accomplished by connecting to an Internet server at a mutually convenient time pre-arranged by email. When it worked well, this facility was invaluable.

However, on numerous occasions the server and Internet connection suffered severe performance problems. This manifested itself by either hanging the program or slowing it down to such an extent that it ceased to be interactive and had to be abandoned at that time. Real-time meetings were also conducted using Internet Relay Chat (IRC). This helped alleviate the performance bottleneck and also provided a slightly more user-friendly graphical user interface. The practical components of the project and the draft and final project reports were exchanged by emailing the URL address of the relevant work, and using a portable document format for the transfer. In the latter stages of the project, Internet Phone took this one step nearer to face-to-face contact by allowing interactive audio, and Microsoft's NetMeeting was used to allow real-time video and audio communication. However, although these should potentially have offered a better means of interacting, poor performance in terms of broken-up sound and jerky video were again the norm at that time.

In sum, whilst on the one hand there was some frustration in getting the tools and services to work and with the poor quality of some of the services, on the other hand the use of email for the bulk of the conversation exchange proved quite adequate, especially when it could be supplemented with IRC. In addition, the use of the WWW enabled immediate viewing of the constructed web pages of educational sites and of the Podiatry test demonstration. Whilst the setting up and use of these communication systems created an additional time overhead in the project that would not have been a factor in the traditional case, without them supervision of the project would not have been not have been practicable within the available time scale.

Case Study 4 - A Demonstration of the Educational Potential of the WWW through a study of Tele-working

The last few years have seen a growth in interest in the concept of distance learning in the field of education and in the use of teleworking to provide a way of conducting work from home. Current predictions suggest that these could become very significant ways of learning and working in future.

It is likely that distance learning will continue its early adoption of many of the existing techniques and technologies used for teleworking. As part of a small-scale study at LMU (Hobbs and Armstrong 1998) an investigation was carried out into the working environment of teleworking, examining the currently debated issues associated with it, and setting out to explore the potential advantages and drawbacks. Although this study was conducted within a business context it is argued that many of the findings are equally applicable within an educational setting.

The term teleworking is often used to encompass a number of different styles of work. For example, it may include people working *at home* (such as programmers), people working *from home* (such as salespeople), and people working *at workcenters* (such as telecottages and satellite offices). Teleworking can bring advantages for the employer, the employee and the environment. It may also provide new job opportunities for the disabled, alleviating some of the effects of immobility. Reid (1993) suggests that cost savings can be achieved through teleworking by reducing the need for centrally maintained offices in expensive locations. Further, Gray et al (1995) and Heap (1995) found teleworkers to be more productive than office bound staff who have to travel to work and tend to suffer a higher level of stress.

Many of the foregoing observations carry over exactly to students who choose a form of teleworking to work on their studies from home or at a distance from the educational institution. Teleworking is generally regarded as a 'green' activity, primarily because of the reduction in travel, the consequent fuel savings and lessening of pressure on congested city centres and overstretched public transport. For the educational institution, distance learning may be seen as a possible way to reduce the increasing pressure on expensive resources of buildings and teaching staff, thereby offering a potential way of running the courses more cost-effectively. As for the student, teleworking reduces travelling time and cost, and probably brings with it greater flexibility in delivery.

The disadvantages to the individual are predominately psychological. In some teleworking scenarios individuals may be totally isolated from interaction with their peers and the institution. This may be either through their own choice as in the case of a writer or musician retreating alone to the mountains to compose, or else through necessity such as a research scientist who is required to take seismic readings for an oil company in a desolate environment such as Antarctica. In the latter case the only contact with others may be through infrequent email messages detailing instructions, and it is in such situations that the effects of social isolation on the individual are likely to be at their most severe.

It would seem vitally important for a socially isolated teleworker that they should be in regular contact with others on a social level and not just through their working or learning environment if they are to stay mentally healthy and continue to perform their work duties efficiently. This social contact may be achieved through using modern technology such as video-conferencing, cellular telephones, fax and electronic mail, all of which should help to lessen the individual's feeling of loneliness. An educational institution offering distance learning to their students will need to be aware of these dangers and ensure that they provide the means to overcome them.

Case Study 5 - A Demonstration of the Educational Potential of the WWW in Collaborative Learning and Problem Solving

One key question associated with teleworking is whether the quality of work using modern teleworking methods such as electronic mail is of a comparable standard with that produced using more traditional face-to-face working practices (Gray et al 1995) and (Reid 1993). It is equally important to ascertain in the case of distance-learning students using teleworking technology. To investigate this issue further, Armstrong (Hobbs and Armstrong 1998) devised two experiments that involved observing a team of three subjects as they worked together in trying to solve a problem. For comparison, they were firstly observed working in a traditional working environment around a table, and then working in isolation from each other using only electronic mail for communication as in a typical teleworking environment.

Both experiments had a set time limit to generate a realistic level of stress as might be found in this situation in the real world. As a measure of the stress levels experienced by the subjects under the two working environments, their pulse rates were taken before and after completion of the tasks in both experiments. In the first experiment, the three subjects were isolated in a room together with a standard survival-type problem-solving exercise – the establishing of importance ratings to fifteen items to a space crew stranded on the moon. The aim was to observe how quickly and successfully the team worked their way towards NASA's recommended solution.

Initially, after having read the problem description, a balanced discussion involving all three participants took place. However, after six minutes of the allotted twenty had passed and the first five most important items had been identified, the discussion changed dramatically. The team began to have difficulty in deciding how the remaining items on the list should be rated, and by the ten-minute mark, one subject had taken the role of a leader and another had withdrawn from the discussion. With five minutes left, the silent member began to contribute again and a more balanced discussion ensued, with voting where necessary, through to completion of the task with thirty seconds to spare.

Although the team's solution was not identical to NASA's, it was very close and acceptable. Pulse rates were found to have increased by eight beats per minute for the two most active subjects representing a sizeable increase, probably attributable to the degree of heated discussion they undertook, and by four beats per minute for the less active one. All three subjects indicated they enjoyed the task and the environment of close proximity working. However, the less active subject claimed he had felt overpowered by the personalities of the other two when the discussions ran into disagreement declaring "... they seemed oblivious to my suggestions so I decided to take a back seat role and leave them to argue it out".

The second experiment was based around a desert survival exercise that again required identification of important items for a team stranded, this time, in the desert. It was devised to ascertain how the three subjects could work together while being isolated from each other and using only electronic mail for communication as in a typical teleworking environment. Subjects worked at networked PCs, each in a separate room so that no visual or verbal communication was possible. A slightly extended time limit of twenty-five minutes was set to allow for the poor performance of the computer network being used.

Exchanging their initial thoughts via the email system they soon established the key features of the problem and offered each other suggestions for the items that should rank high in the importance rating. Within eleven minutes they had correctly identified the five most important items. They then moved to items lower down the list at which point it soon became apparent that they had strongly differing views and some considerable time (eight minutes) was spent with each justifying his own judgement. Eventually agreement reached within the time limit on each item's degree of importance. Apparently this process was aided by the extensive reasoning that had already taken place earlier.

Again, the team was found to have developed a good solution when compared to that of the 'expert'. This time, pulse rates were found to have risen by only two beats per minute for two subjects and by three for the third, a result that suggests the teleworking environment was less stressful, perhaps by being less confrontational. Indeed, no leader emerged throughout this problem solving exercise, and there was generally equal participation. Indeed, the previously less active subject commented that he felt he had had a better opportunity to express his opinions using email.

As far as completing the tasks was concerned, both environments proved to be highly successful in achieving the solving of the problems. The second experiment showed that the teleworking environment facilitated an even distribution of ideas and contributions from all three subjects. Whereas in the face-to-face working a leader had emerged to dominate the discussion, and one member had become overwhelmed by the force of debate, in the teleworking environment the quieter subject was able to contribute on a more equal basis. This might suggest that the teleworking environment encourages broader, more democratic discussion. The face-to-face working environment of the first experiment appeared to be more stressful for the participants, although on balance, this was the style of working that the subjects finally felt they marginally preferred.

Turning now the relevance of this study to an educational environment, it is a fact that the educational systems across the globe are coming under increasing pressure to become more efficient and more flexible to the needs of the learners. In particular, people are increasingly requiring and seeking education or retraining beyond the traditionally assigned ages. Distance education is seen as a possible solution for many of these in that workers can receive in-time training without having to leave work to travel to an educational institution, and foreign students may study in another country without the expense of having to leave their own.

If a tele-education arrangement is to be a success it is important that the potential student has appropriate personal qualities that allow them to work unsupervised or be supervised remotely. These include self-motivation, self-discipline, commitment to learning, adaptability, self-organisation, and ability to work with little social contact.

More generally, working, reporting and communication arrangements between the student, tutors and other students will need to be established, as well as any attendance requirements on the part of the student. Ensuring that the student does not become isolated from the educational institution and other students will probably be a priority. The experimental evidence described above provides some anecdotal evidence that collaborative problem solving, such as often found in group assignment work, can take place adequately or even more effectively using a distance technology such as email. However, occasional attendance at class meetings will go some way towards preventing isolation if this is feasible.

The driving forces that have motivated teleworking are unlikely now to be halted. Likewise the pressures on education worldwide are also unlikely to abate in the near future. Against this, the costs of telecommunications are falling, as is the cost of bandwidth hungry technologies such as video-conferencing. These factors are likely to hasten an evolutionary change in working and learning practices as a long-term consequence of the information technology revolution.

However, in both cases, rather than a sudden change, it is more likely that there will be a gradual, evolutionary change in working and learning practices as a long-term consequence of the information technology revolution. In all probability, teleworking will increasingly be absorbed into the mainstream of normal working practice and tele-education gradually phased in for appropriate groups of students. More flexible, location-independent working and study practices will emerge. It will become accepted practice for workers to spend part of their time working outside the traditional office or studying within it.

Conclusions

Assuming that the future of the WWW is secure, at least for the foreseeable future, it is inevitable that education will stand to benefit as a result of the continuing growth and development of this information-rich environment. The most significant impact is likely to come in the distance education arena where the remote use of advanced teaching materials will reduce costs and enable more students to gain a useful education. The WWW's potential collaborative features will, as they evolve further, offer greater interaction between distance education students.

The practical components of Taylor's project (Section 2 above) demonstrated the large quantity and varying quality of educational material already available on WWW. At this relatively early stage of development of the WWW it is not surprising that a proportion of the published material is not of high quality. However, it is encouraging that many of the visited educational WWW sites were useful and informative. The cataloguing of the enormous variety of educational resources available on-line, and the publishing of these lists are useful and important activities. The continuing compilation of related WWW sites will increase the usability of the WWW in all areas, including education.

The WWW seems particularly well suited to education in a medical area such as Podiatry that is visually intensive. The WWW's inherent multimedia capabilities are well used in such an application, suggesting that its adoption for this kind of teaching environment is a real possibility. The use of the WWW and the Internet for the supervision of this project offered some valuable insights into the problems that may be encountered in the development of WWW-based education. Despite the initial time overheads, it is likely that the increase in demand for distance learning which has already begun may well be satisfied, at least in part, by the types of the WWW functionality discussed in this chapter. Furthermore, the lack of face-to-face communication may be ameliorated in the future by the introduction of affordable, Internet-based, video-conferencing systems.

However, the success of a transition towards a tele-education environments educational homeworking arrangement require careful thought and planning and depend heavily on the motivation of the course tutor and course participants. Students will need to be able to work largely unsupervised with only occasional remote supervision. Communication arrangements between the student, tutors and other students will need to be set up carefully so the student does not feel unduly isolated from the educational institution and the other students. Armstrong's experimental evidence (Section 11 above) suggests that collaborative problem solving of the kind practised by students in group assignment work, can take place adequately or even more effectively using a distance technology such as email. However, if they can be arranged, occasional face-to-face meetings such as summer schools will help alleviate the isolation problems.

Above all, institutional access to the Internet and the WWW in particular must increase dramatically. Governments must propose and support schemes such as the UK Labour Party's initiative to ensure a WWW facility in every school. Universities must realise the potential of the technology and invest in the infrastructure to offer high-quality WWW facilities to every student, again with the required support, and a recognition that the WWW can have a major impact on undergraduate and graduate education. Further development of the cable and telephone infrastructure, and the lowering of call charges will increase the availability of access still further, and as more participants contribute to the WWW the more useful it will become.

References

Baker M. (1994); A Model for Negotiation in Teaching-Learning Dialogues; in *Journal of Artificial Intelligence in Education,* vol. 5 no 2, 199-254.

Bell C. (1996); *A study of the provision of a local map as a navigation tool in a hypertext learning environment*; unpublished BSc thesis, Leeds Metropolitan University.

Blumberg R. B. (1994); *An Electronic Science/Math/History Resource for the WWW,*URL
http://www.ncsa.uiuc.edu/SDG/IT94/Proceedings/Educ/blumberg.mendelweb/MendelWeb94.blumberg.html.

Cho P. (1994); *IntelliTeaching - High Impact Learning*, URL, http://www.ncsa.uiuc.edu/SDG/IT94 /Proceedings/MedEd/cho/ncsa-cho.html.

Curtis P. and Nichols D. (1993); *MUD's Grow UP: Social Virtual Reality in the Real World.* URL, http://lucien.berkeley.edu/MOO/MUDsGrowUp.ps.

Elsom-Cook M. (1989); Guided discovery learning and bounded user modelling; in Self J (ed.) *Artificial Intelligence and Human Learning: Intelligent Computer-aided Instruction*; Chapman and Hall.

Facemyer K. C. (1996); Research on a virtual school: lessons, outcomes, and a model; in *Proceedings of SITE 96 - Seventh International Conference of the Society for Information Technology and teacher Education (SITE)*, p 732-4, 13-16 March 1996, Phoenix, USA.

Fjuk A. and Sorensen H. B. (1996); Drama as a Metaphor for Design of Situated, Collaborative Distributed Learning, in *Proceedings of the Collaborative Virtual Environments Workshop*, University of Nottingham, UK.

Friere P. (1972); *The Pedagogy of the Oppressed*; Penguin.

Girle R. A. (1986); Dialogue and Discourse; in Bishop G. and Van Lint W. (eds.), *Proceedings of the Fourth Annual Computer Assisted Learning in Tertiary Education Conference, Adelaide* 1986, distributed by Office of Continuing Education, University of Adelaide.

Gray M. et al. (1995), *Teleworking Explained*, John Wiley and Sons.

Hartley J. R. (1993); Interacting with multimedia; in *University Computing* No 15.

Heap N. (1995), *Information Technology and Society*, Sage Publications Ltd.

Hobbs D. J. and Armstrong J. (1998), An Experimental Study of Social and Psychological Aspects of Teleworking: The Implications for Tele-Education, in *Proceedings of WebNet98*, Association for the Advancement of Computers in Education, ISBN 1-880094-31-2, pp440-445, Orlando, USA.

Hobbs D. J. and Moore D. J. (1992); Instructional Technology for Student-Centred Learning: the Leeds Polytechnic Experience; in *Proceedings of the International Interactive Multimedia Symposium*, Perth 1992.

Hobbs D. J. and Taylor R. J. (1998), Distance Learning Across the Internet - An Examination of the Potential of Electronic Networking to Provide Effective Virtual Educational Environments, in *Proceedings of 4th International NETIES 98 Conference*, pp 15-19, Leeds, UK.

Hutchings G. A., Carr L. A. and Hall W. (1992); STACKMAKER: an environment for creating hypermedia learning materials; in *Hypermedia 4*, no 3, pp 197-211

Ibrahim B (1994); Distance Learning with the World Wide Web; *in Proceedings of the International Conference on Open and Distance Learning - Critical Success Factors*, Geneva, 10-12 October 1994, pp 255-265.

Ibrahim B. and Franklin S. D. (1995); Advanced Educational Uses of the World-Wide Web; *In Proceedings of Third World Wide Web Conference - WWW 95*, Darmstadt, Germany, April 10-14 1995, vol 27, pp 871--877.

Laurillard D. (1995); Multimedia and the Changing Experience of the Learner; in *British Journal of Educational Technology*, Vol 26, No 3, pp 179-189.

Moore D. J. and Hobbs D. J. (1997); Strategies for the Introduction of Multimedia Systems, in *Social and Organisational Issues Dimension of Information Systems* (eds. Orange G, Katsikides S), McGraw-Hill (in press for 1997).

Moore D. J. and Hobbs D. J. (1994), Towards an intelligent tutoring system for educational debate, in *Proceedings of the Interdisciplinary Workshop on Complex Learning in Computer Environments*, Joensuu, Finland.

Moyse R. and Elsom-Cook M. T. (1992); Knowledge negotiation: An Introduction; in Moyse R, Elsom-Cook M T (eds.) *Knowledge Negotiation*; Academic Press.

Mullier D. J. (1995a); A Hybrid Connectionist/Knowledge-Based Approach to Intelligent Tutoring with Hypermedia, in *Proceedings of the Aspects of Educational Technology 95 Conference*, Plymouth.

Mullier D. J. (1995b); Using a Neural Network to Model Hypermedia Browsing: An Alternative to Traditional Intelligent Tutoring Methods, in *Proceedings of the Hypermedia in Sheffield 95 Conference*, Sheffield.

Nielsen J. (1990); The art of navigating in hypertext; in *Communications of the ACM*, 33:3 pp296-310.

Nielsen J. (1993); *HYPERtext and HYPERmedia*, Academic Press, London, UK.

Nkambou R. and Gauthier G. (1996); Integrating WWW Resources in an Intelligent Tutoring System; in *Journal of Network and Computer Applications* vol. 19 no 4 October 1996 353-365.

Norman K. L. (1994); Navigating the educational space with HYPERCOURSEWARE, in *Hypermedia 6*, no 1, pp 35-60.

Perron D. (1994); *Learning on the WWW: A Case Study*; URL, http://www.ncsa.uiuc.edu/SDG/IT94/Proceedings/Educ/perron/perron.html.

Reid, A. (1993), Teleworking as a Guide to Good Practice, NCC Blackwell.

Russell D. B. and Baird J. H. (1995); *WWW, Researchers and Research Services*; URL, http://www.scu.edu.au/ausweb95/papers/index.html#RTFToC65.

Self J. (1992); Computational Viewpoints; in Moyse R., Elsom-Cook M. T. (eds.) *Knowledge Negotiation*; Academic Press.

Skillcorn D. B. (1996); Using Distributed Hypermedia for Collaborative learning in Universities, in *The Computer Journal*, vol. 39, no 6, 471-482.

Trathern C. and Sajeev A. S. M. (1996); A Protocol for Computer Mediated Education Across the Internet", *British Journal of Educational Technology* vol. 27 no 3 204-213.

Treloar A. (1995); *Electronic Scholarly Publishing and the World Wide Web*; URL, http://www.scu.edu.au/ausweb95/papers/index.html#RTFToC55.

6 Demonstration of how Soft Systems Methodology can be used to Structure the Issues Associated with Distance Learning Activities

BARBARA HOWELL AND NIMAL JAYARATNA
SHEFFIELD HALLAM UNIVERSITY, UK

Introduction

Information and communications technologies have evolved dramatically and dynamically providing little time to absorb and generate technologically coherent learning paradigms. In addition, there is growing demand for tertiary education and political pressure for better-educated citizens. Education as we know it is in a state of transformation. Change is inevitable if institutions are to provide a quality service to a wider audience, from different social and work related backgrounds, influenced by government proposals for increased competition in global markets, improved productivity and effective use of resources.

Virtual-U is an environment created by Simon Frazer University of Canada (SFU) to facilitate students learning through distance learning modes, irrespective of where they are located. In this sense, it is providing access to a University for potential students, which can exist in a virtual sense closest to the students learning environment. To enable Distance Learning (DL) evolution a research exercise was undertaken with participants from the United Kingdom and Canada, mainly academics involved in the development, use and assessment of the effectiveness of this mode of learning.

First named author of this chapter actively participated in this research exercise, assessing its facilities and suitability for the development of DL materials. This chapter evaluates the experience of being involved in this exercise. The evaluation suggests the need for clarity of objectives and rationale for a virtual university because of embedded notions. The chapter proposes the use of Soft Systems Methodology (SSM) for structuring the set of design activities. It demonstrates an example of the activities that can be undertaken in order for each group of participants to develop specific DL applications.

Virtual-U Environment

A collaborative arrangement was established between SFU, the Open University (OU) and Sheffield Hallam University (SHU). The exercise comprised a twelve-week course (start date 20th Jan 1998) dedicated to the investigation of virtual education, with approximately fifty-three participants from the three institutions. The environment to be used for the exercise was Virtual-U software, developed by SFU, which operates on a Web browser (see fig 1) and offers asynchronous communication.

Virtual-U supports the performance of core activities including course design, individual and group learning, knowledge structuring, class management, and evaluation. The concept of the exercise was to enable participants to learn about Tele-Learning by engaging in it. Indicative content included approaches to Tele-Learning, design and implementation of online teaching, lessons learned from online teaching, technological issues and evaluation and vision of online teaching.

The course allowed participants from the three institutions to interact and collaborate with each other and the facilitators. It encouraged both individual and group work in the investigation and construction of Tele-learning environments. It was also envisaged that participants would have basic skills in the use of email, Netscape Navigator and preferably some experiences relative to Computer Mediated Conferencing (CMC). However, participants learned to work online by engaging in seminars, discussion groups and collaborating in research projects over the Internet.

In order to abstract the issues and experiences, the rest of the chapter will be organised under the following headings; learning curve and commitment; social cues and isolation; asynchronous text based communications.

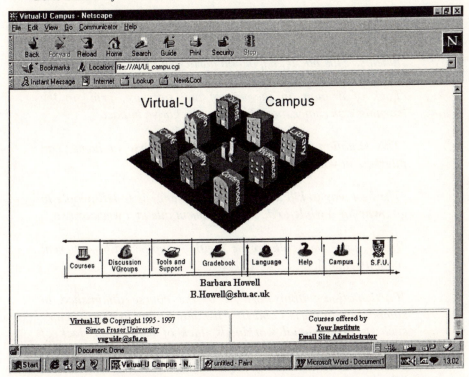

Figure 1 Virtual-U Environment (screen shot reproduced with the permission of Linda Harasim of Simon Frazer University)

Learning Curve and Commitment

The learning curve was quite steep and difficulties at the beginning of a course of study could hinder continual commitment. Insecurity, uncertainty and lack of social atmosphere all contribute to the erosion of self-belief when using embryonic modes in solitude. Gerard Prendergast (1997) maintains, 'There is an initial learning curve for students, who are unfamiliar with computers or computer conferencing… There can be technical difficulties to overcome, but these are diminishing with the latest software… This medium has a real telepresence and it takes a few weeks for most students/tutors to adapt to the difference in the communication style of CMC… Time management can be problematic for both student and tutors'. The medium can also inhibit those who lack self-confidence to participate (Harasim, 1996). The participants confirmed these observations.

Comments made by participants of the Virtual-U include:

"The learning curve with the Virtual-U varied amongst the students. This had an impact on participation and motivation."

"Lack of training in the use of any software, prior to the learning experience, possibly have a negative impact."
.
"This situation, in which you have the course at home, can interfere in your life"

"The best way to kill a computer conference is to tell people to go away for a while to do an assignment due in a week or two."

"How can we collaborate with people with different commitments?"

"Participation within Part III of the course diminished in comparison to Parts I and II. This may be due to many factors such as professional workloads, lack of motivation, lack of direction etc."

"On line learning is tremendously time and labour intensive and requires a serious commitment from both the instructor AND the learner."

"I recognise that cultural differences in style, in choice of comments, subjects, background experience (not knowledge) could, eventually, create more difficulties than solve the ones that inspired my collaborative attempt."

Comment made by Virtual-U Facilitator:

"The slow response times and hence access difficulties are having a negative impact upon users' ability to navigate and investigate the system, and engage in discussions."

On completion of the twelve-week course nine conferences relating to the topics under discussion or assignments, had taken place. The participants could also submit comments to the Welcome, Help, Café and personal conference areas. The first two conferences TL Designs and TL

Designs: 1A The Virtual-U (reference 9 & 10 in figure 2), attracted the most interest with sixty-one and seventy submissions respectively. The third and fourth conferences (reference 12 & 13 in figure 2) attracted thirty-nine and seventeen submissions respectively. It is also interesting to note, only six out of fifty-three participants and sixteen major contributors participated in the final discussions.

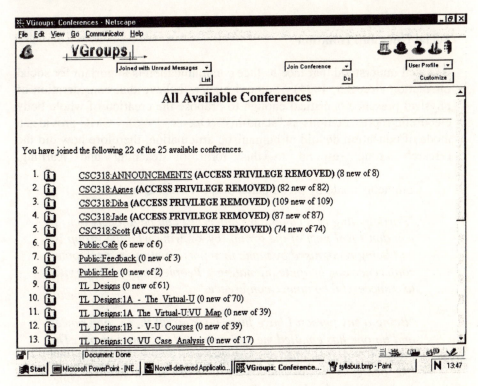

Figure 2 Virtual-U Conference area (screen shot reproduced with the permission of Linda Harasim of Simon Frazer University)

Technical difficulties, social culture of participants, aims and objectives, course content and facilitator role all played a part in the participant's commitment to the exercise. In an environment whereby contributions are essential to the ethos of the medium, variable commitments of the participants provided inequality of submissions. In addition, the medium is described as labour intensive requiring an appreciation of both the facilitator and participant role. For example how many hours are required by the instructors to successfully facilitate a program and are the learners heavily involved in domestic, work or social activities? In effect, what demands will be placed on the facilitator and the target audience by this mode of teaching and learning? The diversity of contents, in which the learners operate, is a significant factor in the effectiveness of learning.

Social Cues and Isolation

It is well understood that face-to-face communication is important for social interaction (Keegan, 1994). Some designers believe that consideration of physical presence is critical enough to propose the creation of whole body electronic representations as "stand-ins" (Oravec, 1996). CMC provides a mode of education devoid of humanistic articulation, therefore how did the research group respond to this form of teaching and learning.

Comments made by participants of the Virtual-U include:

"Participating in a computer conference can be a lonely act. If you don't feel part of the group (by knowing who the group is) and being recognised by name then participating in a computer conference can be quite alienating... People's inputs are so vital to a successful computer conference."

"Being a shy person I have hung back on all these conferences and no one has emailed me with words of encouragement. The problem is that no one is talking to me and reassuring me.... It's like being in prison and trying to learn about the world by looking through a key hole."

" I experienced sensory deprivation through not being able to see the real people and their body language in this class."

"I want to know who I am embarrassing myself in front of."

"The mutual pleasure of seeing and being seen. This is more than just video viewing - this is human mutuality that is deep in our experience, right from the week we were born when we gazed with mum and learned to touch and be touched... To lose

this kind of human interaction, and to become only projectors of words, ahh, what a terrible loss, truly a grief."

"I realise how much I was bound to the need of having continuous reinforcement of the feeling of being accepted in social groups. In face-to-face situations, you get it by glances, comments, touches, laughs, etc... The online environment was a desert for me in the beginning."

Social interactions can be fundamental to the learning process. However face-to-face depravation can focus effort more purposefully (Oravec, 1996). Software has been specifically developed to overcome the visual dilemma of computer conferencing[1], but this investigation was not intended to draw comparisons between the mediums, rather to clarify issues for consideration. Many Virtual-U participants commented on the lack of visual contact and social interaction. Lack of personal cues, which illustrate meaning, help interpretation, and influence the intentions of the message were seen as demanding for the novice users. The dynamics of existing software, be it text based, voice or video conferencing, must relay the message effectively and exploit the medium in relation to overall learning objectives. In addition, the role of facilitator should complement the medium in terms of counselling and encouraging participation.

Asynchronous Text Based Communications

Benefits of CMC include bringing together like-minded individuals who are geographically dispersed and operating in different time zones. According to Tiffin and Rajasingham (1995), 'An advantage of an educational system as an international network is the variety of courses that could be accessed and the opportunities to link with like-minded learners around the world. This is a vision of the kind of educational system that could become possible in an information society, a virtual network of learners, teachers, knowledge and examples of the problems the learners want to solve'. The medium allows participants to communicate at a time most convenient to them. Marold and Larsen (1996) illustrate the benefits as, 'The new CMC media have the ability to overcome time as a variable affecting the communication process. For example, you could send a computer message

---

[1] http://cu-seeme-cornell.edu - CU- SeeMe software
http://www.ibm.com/sfasp/p2p.htm - IBM Person to Person software
http://www.microsoft.com/netmeeting/ - Microsoft NetMeeting software

from New York at 8 am to a person in California where it would be 5 am, a time most people are not receptive to phone calls.' Virtual-U participants clearly recognise these factors as a positive feature of global educational systems.

Comments made by participants of the Virtual-U include:

"The task of getting students from three different institutions linked across six time zones to take a course lead by four different professors is an amazing feat which just a few years ago would have been impossible.... We got to work with people from two countries, sharing thoughts."

"I enjoyed the chance to take a course that attempted to bridge large geographical and knowledge distances and bring different perspectives and experiences to bear."

"The great advantage of this medium is asynchronicity, I can, we all can, join anytime."

It is also widely recognised that for certain populations, text based communications enable equality of participation (McComb, 1993), provide greater access to women, minorities and other disadvantaged learners. These positive aspects are further emphasised by Mason (1992), 'because we cannot see one another, we are unable to form prejudices about others before we read what they have to say. Race, gender, age, national origin and physical appearance are not apparent unless a person wants to make such characteristics public. People whose physical handicaps make it difficult to form new friendships find that virtual communities treat them as they always wanted to be treated - as transmitters of ideas and feeling beings, not carnal vessels with a certain appearance and way of walking and talking (or not walking and talking).' These assertions are confirmed by the participants of the research exercise as plausible benefits of text based modes of education.

Comments made by participants of the Virtual-U include:

"One of the unique opportunities that online course environments provides us with is the chance to voice an opinion, an idea, a concept and to have other build on it .... As equals, instructors and students alike."

"VU presents students with a genuine equal opportunity to contribute to the discussions. In face-to-face, the initial contributions sets the agenda and it can be very difficult to deviate from this."

"This has been a unique opportunity for me to participate as equal with a peer group."

Comment made by Virtual-U Facilitator:

"The asynchronous nature of the online environment leads to a more reflective, 'abiding' experience - the mulling over of issues."

"Communication research shows that text is a more mindful medium than video, which is more effective (i.e., the difference between reading about a war, and seeing a TV view: text encourages more objective responses, view more emotional-visceral responses)."

The main disadvantage of computer mediated conferencing for the learner is the extreme difficulty in putting the written word into context. As Collins (1996) states, 'Part of the risk of loss of meaning rests in the skill of the sender in using the technologies involved in the transformation process - a skilled writer does better with her word processor than a less-talented writer - and much effort has gone into the process of making our "idea-transformation" technologies as helpful as possible to allow us to express ourselves as we intended.' In addition, the prolonged discourse associated with asynchronous communications (Mason, 1995), irritates the impatient. Hiltz and Toroff (1993) found, 'There are tremendous elements of frustration involved in this lack of immediacy. Often, a person wants an answer to response now, and the minutes go by and nothing happens'. Yet again, previous research has noted problematic areas, which reflect the observations of the Virtual-U participants.

Comments made by participants of the Virtual-U include:

"With Tele-learning it is easy to stop. You just don't bother to log on. It is difficult to feel that you are offending anyone or letting people down."

"It's not just that I'm late contributing to the conference, I really feel quite intimidated by the prospect of doing so. Typing up a contribution seems so much more formal than just making a verbal comment."

"The exclusive use of writing was an enormous personal challenge for me. I thought I was prepared for the experience by having almost one year of studies in my bag but it was, really, a big illusion."

It is clear that participants appreciated the experience of communicating with distant peer groups via Virtual-U. With technologies advancing at such a pace, the process of teaching and learning can now operate more efficiently as a global education system. Asynchronous communications can also support more carefully thought out debates with composed and reflective contributions, hence an aid to critical thought processes. However, text based modes proved challenging to even the more experienced users, with some reticent to commit to the word processor. Typical problems include the formality of the medium and the lack of personal response. According to Sorby (1992), 'Insecure social climate and uncertainty about framework, norms and written communication, are factors to consider when planning courses using computer conferencing.' The issues would therefore revolve around the synergy between educational modes and the facilitators' roles. In addition, was 'global participation' found to be a satisfactory learning outcome for the instigators? Have the aims and objectives of the course been met by using this form of technology?

Case for a New Approach

Given the diverse and qualitative nature of the feedback from the Virtual-U participants, the usual way of responding to this form of feedback is to modify or change what is possible and ignore those comments that are beyond one's control (e.g. How can we collaborate with people with different commitments?). Another way to legitimise feedback is to devise a questionnaire that will enable participants to comment on specified topics. This means that the questions have to be pre-formulated by the developer of the questionnaire. In both cases, the approach taken is piece-meal and pragmatic and may indeed vary dependant on the reactions of the course team. However, there is a methodology that takes 'perceptions' and viewpoints as central to its transformation activities. This is known as SSM (Checkland, 1996; Checkland and Scholes, 1997; Checkland and Holwell, 1997).

Application of SSM to Clarify the Role of Distance Learning

Many studies have been conducted that concentrate on specific elements of CMC (Ferris, 1996; Kirkwood, 1995; Morgan, 1995). However it is well documented that for CMC to succeed in education a more holistic approach is required (Waggoner, 1992; Metz, 1994). The emergent properties of distance learning systems and the appreciation of classifying CMC initiatives as human activity systems require a methodological approach that uses epistemological notions (Checkland, 1996; Jayaratna, 1994). SSM is a methodology that has been developed and used for resolution of 'problem situations' over that last twenty-five years (Checkland, 1996; Checkland and Scholes, 1997; Checkland and Holwell, 1997). Its epistemology has been and continues to be one of 'learning'. This means that the methodology used needs to leave behind knowledge in the participants not only of the results, from the use of SSM, but also the way to use SSM so that the participants are able to continue with their learning (Checkland and Scholes, 1997; Checkland and Holwell, 1997; Jayaratna, 1994).

SSM can be used in two different modes. Mode one is a seven-stage methodology (see figure 3), which uses participants and their 'world views' as central to its application. Unlike other methodologies that marginalise or ignore opinions/statements that cannot be substantiated or rationalised, SSM incorporates these viewpoints as central to the discussion that it attempts to generate. In figure 3, step one is the introduction of the methodology user to a situation in which 'problems' are perceived. SSM does not take problems for solving but takes an interest in people who see the situation as problematic. This means that it is their views that have to be explored, as they may not see the situation in the same way as the other stakeholders or even agree as to the nature of the 'problems'.

During step two, these views are given legitimacy by capturing them in a 'rich picture'. 'Rich pictures' as the name implies, try to accommodate a wide range of data which other forms of representations exclude. For example, in data flow diagrams only formal flows of data are recorded. Other information concerned with judgement, informal connections and familiarity with customer's etc. is ignored. 'Rich pictures', which usually take diagrammatic and text form, capture viewpoints, feelings, concerns, issues for debate etc. in addition to quantifiable data. The viewpoints, concerns, issues and feelings are given a central role in the methodology.

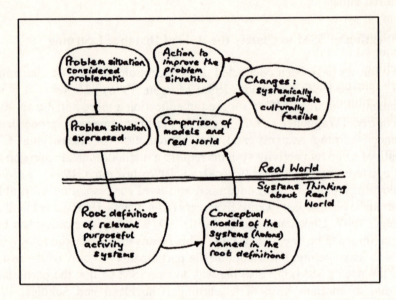

Figure 3 Seven stage model

In step three, many recorded viewpoints/issues are abstracted and given legitimacy. They may very well be radically opposing viewpoints. This legitimacy is achieved by proposing 'notional systems' to realise the viewpoints. For example, in the context of distance learning programmes, a student may view the programme as no more than the delivery of existing course notes on electronic media at a disproportionate cost. This viewpoint can be given legitimacy as in figure 4. In SSM terms, the student takes on the role of a "problem owner". Of course, there can be many such 'problem owners'.

> *"A Distance Learning system owned by the university to exploit the vulnerability of a geographically dispersed group of students by providing existing teaching material via the WEB for qualification and thereby generating additional income for the university".*

Figure 4 Distance Learning system to exploit new markets

Of course, the proposal of such a system would generate sufficient debate in order to bring out the arguments as to why such a view should not be the case. These help to clarify the uncertainties and bring structure to ill-structured situations (Jayaratna, 1994). The expression of such a 'notional system' in written form is described as a 'Root Definition'. In step four, these 'Root Definitions' are extended, by considering the elements that may be required to realise the design notional system. This is called conceptual modelling. In step five, the 'Root Definition' and the associated conceptual models are used as a means of generating debate from which an agreed 'Root Definition' may emerge for development. Step six is where feasible and desirable options are explored, which are then put into action in stage seven. Relevance of a 'notional system' at a theoretical level is established at step five, while the evaluation of its use in practice takes place after step seven.

In mode two, an experienced SSM user may construct a methodology for a particular situation using elements from SSM and other methodologies.

Demonstration of the Applicability of SSM

Here we give an example of the adaptability of SSM. Given that we already have a considerable number of qualitative expressions we could select some of these 'problem owners' and give legitimacy to their expressions by developing 'Root Definitions'. For example, if one of the comments submitted in the conference area is taken in isolation, "I experienced sensory deprivation through not being able to see the real people and their body language in this class". Figure 5 will represent a possible 'Root Definition' based on the worldview of that particular problem owner.

> *"University management owned system, facilitated by academics to provide computer mediated conferencing to geographically dispersed students, using readily available software which ensures isolation of participants".*

Figure 5 Root Definition - Computer Conferencing

The following represents the 'Weltanschauung' (world view), as derived from the first named author's experience of participating in the

Virtual-U research exercise and the comments made by the Virtual-U participants. In this type of provision of education, the 'Root Definition' may need to satisfy the needs of the student population, establish appropriate mode and suitable educational material for providing a facilitator based service. A 'Root Definition' that captures this desire could be illustrated as in figure 6.

> *"A University owned system for providing a computer mediated conferencing environment to a potential student population spread over a wide geographical area, by taking into account financial constraints, educational mode, subject matter, new technologies, facilitator role, social trends and the economic climate."*

Figure 6 Root Definition - Computer Mediated Conferencing System

The root definition is then explored in order to develop conceptual models that would enable the root definition to be realised in practice. The conceptual model is derived from expressing the main operations to bring about the core activity 'provide computer mediated conferencing'. Figure 7 illustrates such an example for the chosen root definition, in figure 6.

Figure 7 provides a graphical representation of the 'system' as a whole, 'provide computer mediated learning system'. Each operation identifies aspects for consideration when developing distance learning initiatives.

For example:

> ➢ *Appreciate social and economic environment* - Do employers want training in the work place? (Life long learning) If women or househusbands wish to return to work are they expected to enter the job market with different skills? Are more school leavers going to University? How will they be funded etc?

> ➢ *Identify student population* - What courses do they want? How do they want to learn? Where do they want to learn? Is one age group, gender, culture in need of distance learning etc?

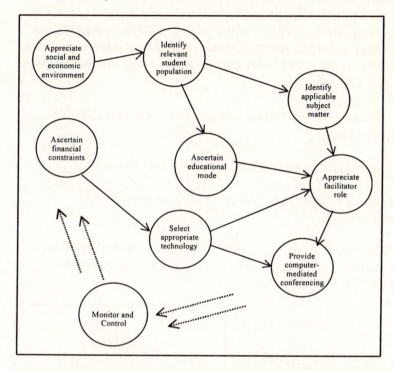

Figure 7 Conceptual Model - Computer Mediated Conferencing
System

➤ *Identify applicable subject matter* - What level is required -
HND, BSc or MSc? What subject - business theory,
numerical analysis or programming etc.?

➤ *Ascertain educational mode* - What methods should be used,
lectures, seminars or tutorial? What mode video
conferencing or text based conferencing etc?

➤ *Appreciate facilitator role* - How much time is needed to
facilitate a computer mediated conference? What skills are
required etc?

➤ *Ascertain financial constraints* - What funds are available
for distance learning initiatives?

➤ *Select appropriate technology* - What software, hardware or
operating system is to be used etc?

SSM is a cyclic process of enquiry and as such the model is completed by monitor and control activities. If the process is implemented the model should be tested for efficiency (the output relative to the resources used), effectiveness (does the system meet the overall aims) and efficacy (does the system work). For example:

> Efficiency - Is the method cost effective? Within reasonable time scales?

> Effectiveness - What is take up, retention and pass rate?

> Efficacy - Does the system provide computer-mediated education?

The conceptual model in figure 7 can be further decomposed to explore second level activities. Figure 8 illustrates an example of the way to appreciate the role of a facilitator.

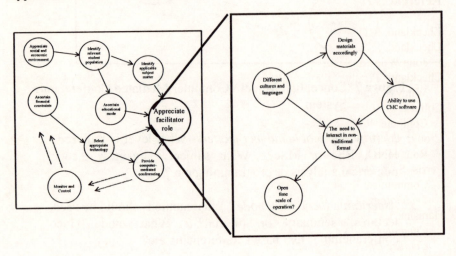

Figure 8 Level 2 - Conceptual Model - Appreciate facilitator role

Conclusions

The chapter discussed the experiences arising from the participation in a distance learning experiment. The use of Virtual-U environment for education provides considerable opportunities and access facilities for a large number of potential individuals who would otherwise not be able to benefit from a university education. However, this medium requires a different level and type of educational mode, facilitator role, technologies and an appreciation of the circumstances and expectations of the learners. The chapter focused on participants feedback which will usually be taken into account in the re-design of programmes in a piecemeal way. The chapter introduced the reader to SSM which takes these qualitative aspects e.g. viewpoint and perceptions as central to its transformation role. It then demonstrates how the use of SSM could help to re-define the role of such distance learning programmes.

References

Checkland, P. (1996) *Systems Thinking, Systems Practice.* John Wiley & Sons.

Checkland, P & Holwell, S. (1997) *Information, Systems and Information Systems.* John Wiley & Sons.

Checkland, P., and Scholes, J. (1997) *Soft Systems Methodology in Action.* John Wiley & Sons.

Collins, B. (1996) *Tele-learning. In a Digital World.* International Thomson Computer Press. London. p 29-75.

Crook, C. (1996) *Computers and the Collaborative Experience of Learning.* Routledge, London.

Ferris, S. P. (1996) Women On-line: Cultural and Relational aspects of Women's Communication in On-line discussion Groups. *Interpersonal Computing and Technology.* **4**, No. 3-4 29-40.

Harasim, L. (1996) Online Education. In: Harrison, M. T., and Stephen, T. (Ed.), *Computer Networking and Scholarly Communication in the Twenty-First-Century University.* State University of New York Press. p. 203-214.

Hiltz, S. R., and Toroff, M. (1993) *The Network Nation.* MIT Press. p. 7-42.

Jayaratna, N. (1994) Understanding *and Evaluating Methodologies.* McGraw-Hill, London.

Keegan, D. (1994) *Otto Peters on Distance education. The Industrialization of Teaching and Learning.* Routledge, London. p. 220-224.

Kirkwood, A. (1995) Over the threshold: Media Technologies for Home Learning. In: Lockwood, F. (Ed.), *Open and Distance Learning Today.* Routledge, London. p. 129-138.

Marold, K. A., and Larsen, G. (1996) *Beyond the Internet.* International Thomson Publishing Company. p. 1-31.

Mason, R. (1992) *Computer Conferencing, The last word...* Beach Holme, Publishing Ltd, Victoria, British Columbia. p. 103-108.

Mason, R. (1995) *Using Communications Media in Open and Flexible Learning.* Kogan Page Ltd, London. p. 11-24.

McComb, M. (1993) Augmenting a group discussion course with computer-mediated communication in a small college setting. *Interpersonal Computing and Technology.* 1, No. 3.

Metz, J. M. (1994) Computer-Mediated Communication: Literature review of a new context. *Interpersonal Computing and Technology.* **2**, No. 2 31-49.

Morgan, A. R. (1995) Student Learning and Students experiences: Research, Theory and Practice. In: Lockwood, F. (Ed.), *Open and Distance Learning Today.* Routledge, London. p. 55-66.

Oravec, J. A. (1996) *Virtual Individuals, Virtual Groups, Human Dimensions of Groupware and Computer Networking.* Cambridge University Press. p. 148-188.

Prendergast, G. (1997) Using Computer-Mediated Communication to Develop Supervisory Skills. In: Armstrong, S, Thompson, G and Brown, S. (Ed.), *Facing up to Radical Changes in Universities and Colleges.* Kogan Page. p. 29-50.

Sorby, M. (1992) Waiting for Electropolis. In: Kaye, A. R. (Ed.), *Collaborative learning through computer conferencing. The Najaden chapters.* NATO ASI Series F: Computer and Systems Sciences, vol. 90. Berlin: Springer-Verlag. p. 39-49.

Tiffin, J., and Rajasingham, L. (1995) *In Search of the Virtual Class.* Routledge, London. p. 1-18.

Waggoner, M. (1992) A Case Study Approach to Evaluation of Computer Conferencing. In: Kaye, A. R. (Ed.), Collaborativ*e learning through computer conferencing. The Najaden chapters.* NATO ASI Series F: Computer and Systems Sciences, vol. 90. Berlin: Springer-Verlag. p.137-146.

7 University21 - An Integrated Educational System

JIANHUA MA AND RUNHE HUANG
THE UNIVERSITY OF AIZU, JAPAN
TOSIYASU L.KUNII, HOSEI UNIVERSITY, JAPAN

Abstract

This chapter proposes a new framework and architecture for designing and developing networked computer based integrated educational systems. With this framework and architecture, a prototype of the integrated educational system (IES), University21, has been developed. University21 consists of five types of virtual rooms: virtual administration office, virtual private office, virtual courseroom, virtual collaboration room and virtual laboratory. Functions and tools associated with each type of rooms are presented and discussed in detail. Many examples are given to show our design ideas and demonstrate how the system functions. University21 is the first integrated educational system designed to support almost all teaching/learning activities towards the goal of global teaching and learning. It can be used by different scales of educational organizations ranging from an individual teacher or professional to a large virtual university.

Introduction

In recent years, advances in multimedia computing, networking and Internet technologies have brought about an educational revolution, i.e., global teaching and learning. So long as their computers are connected to the Internet, teachers and students can conduct teaching/learning activities irrespective of their global positions. This revolution has had a great impact on traditional schools and universities and opens an opportunity to create a new style of school and university, called virtual schools and virtual universities.

Facing the coming of the educational revolution in the human history, a fundamental and challenging problem is the establishment of a standard and unified networked computer based *integrated educational system* (IES) for systematically supporting all teaching and learning activities in real and virtual schools and universities of the future. However, most current computer assisted educational systems [1] - [5] support only a small subset of the activities in a school or university. Only a few research projects have been focused on developing integrated systems, such as Virtual-U [6], Web-CT [7], WCB [8], Learning Space [9], and Top Class [10]. Even so these systems only support teaching and learning of online courses. It is apparent that there are more activities beyond just teaching and learning courses in schools and universities. For example, administration of staff, teachers, students and visitors, management of course-learning orientated laboratories, supervision of undergraduate, MSc and PhD research, and support of collaborative team or group work. University21 under development is a networked computer-based integrated educational system that aims to support all activities in a school or university via networks including the Internet.

As University21 is the first development effort of an IES for truly supporting all school/university activities, the research has to start from definition of the IES and design of its framework. One of our basic ideas is that the concept of the IES is relative and depends upon the scale of a targeted educational provider or organization. The chapter clarifies relations of the IES with scales of educational organizations as well as richness of educational tools. To cover all scales of virtual universities, we propose a general framework that consists of several layers among which the tool layer and the room layer are of primary importance. A variety of rooms are constructed on the room layer based on the tool layer that includes a set of toolkits for supporting administration, course, collaboration, virtual instrument, database management, and system maintenance, respectively. Our previous project, CHEER (Computer-based Hyper-Environment for Educational Reform), was mainly focused on the development of the toolkits at the tool layer [11]-[16]. Current work in the University21 project has been mainly devoted to design and implementation of the five types of virtual rooms on the room layer: virtual administration office, virtual private office, virtual courseroom, virtual collaboration room, and virtual laboratory. These five types of virtual rooms will be further combined to construct different scales of virtual schools/universities.

University21 differs from other systems in the following ways: (1) it supports a wider range of activities beyond just teaching online courses in a school/university. (2) It provides a virtual private office for each registered user (staff, teacher or student) to manage personal activities and data and to enter other virtual rooms. (3) The hyper-environment architecture of virtual courserooms allows many simultaneous activities related to an online course. (4) A new desktop groupware system, the virtual collaboration room (VCR), is incorporated to support a variety of advanced collaborative activities, such as meeting, tele-lecturing, group project, team work, student instruction and informal chat. (5) Any scale of virtual schools/universities can be built by flexibly assembling and customizing the rooms since each room is designed and implemented as a relatively independent unit.

The rest of this chapter is organized as follows: Section 2 presents our thoughts and considerations regarding the concept, the general framework, the design criteria and architecture of an integrated educational system. The chapter then takes four sections to discuss functions and implementations of the different types of rooms in University21: virtual administration office, virtual private office, virtual courseroom, virtual collaboration room and virtual laboratory, respectively. Finally, conclusions are drawn and future work is addressed in Section 7.

Concept, Framework, Criteria and Architecture in Developing Integrated Educational Systems

The teaching and learning process involves many activities. An educational system should be able to provide a variety of functions to support these activities. Depending on functions a system provides, the system can be classified as a single function system, multiple function system or integrated educational system. Developing integrated educational systems is considered as one of the important research directions in the area of networked computer based teaching/learning. Although there has been and continues to be much research and development, some fundamental issues, such as the definition of an IES, a framework for IES, criteria and architecture of developing an IES, are still unclear. After two years' experience of designing and developing the integrated educational system, University21, we would like to present our thoughts and considerations regarding the fundamental issues. The definition, framework, criteria, and architecture we present may be incomplete, but this research is the first effort to systematically clarify them.

Given that a precise definition of IES is not easy, it has, however, been noticed that the following three factors are associated with the concept of an IES as illustrated in Figure 1.

- the quantity and the quality of functions
- the scale of educational organization
- the richness of tools.

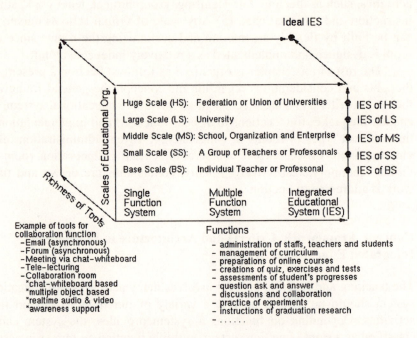

Ideal IES

Scales of Educational Org.		IES
Huge Scale (HS):	Federation or Union of Universities	IES of HS
Large Scale (LS):	University	IES of LS
Middle Scale (MS):	School, Organization and Enterprise	IES of MS
Small Scale (SS):	A Group of Teachers or Professonals	IES of SS
Base Scale (BS):	Individual Teacher or Professonal	IES of BS

Single Function System | Multiple Function System | Integrated Educational System (IES)

Richness of Tools

Example of tools for collaboration function
- Email (asynchronous)
- Forum (asynchronous)
- Meeting via chat–whiteboard
- Tele–lecturing
- Collaboration room
  * chat–whiteboard based
  * multiple object based
  * realtime audio & video
  * awareness support

Functions
- administration of staffs, teachers and students
- management of curriculum
- preparations of online courses
- creations of quiz, exercises and tests
- assessments of student's progresses
- question ask and answer
- discussions and collaboration
- practice of experiments
- instructions of graduation research
- ......

Figure 1 Integrated educational systems in relation to scales of educational organisation, functions and tools

An integrated educational system should have rich tools and a large quantity of functions that are well integrated in such a natural way as to effectively support various teaching/learning activities. However, 'rich tools', 'a large quantity of functions' and 'well integrated' are relative and associated with scales of educational organization. For different scales of educational organization, the corresponding IES scale varies with its requirements and criteria. An IES may be designed for the following five scales of educational organization:

Base Scale (BS): The educational organization is an individual teacher or professional who provides an on-line course on his/her specialty.

Small Scale (SS): The educational organization is a group of teachers or professionals who join together to provide a set of on-line courses on a specified subject.

Middle Scale (MS): The educational organization is a school, organization or enterprise that provides a series of teaching/learning activities for their students or employees on some subjects.

Large Scale (LS): The educational organization is a university that conducts all teaching, learning and managing activities on many subjects.

Huge Scale (HS): The educational organization is a federation or union of virtual universities.

Functions provided in an IES vary depending upon the scale of a target educational organization. For example, it may be enough for an IES of the base scale to have the functions of online course authoring, asynchronous communications based on email and homework management, while an IES of the large scale must include many more functions, such as the functions listed in Figure 1. Generally, an IES of a larger scale is more complex than an IES of a smaller scale. When developing or evaluating an IES, we must first specify the scale of educational organization the system is designed for.

Each function of an IES is supported by a tool or a set of tools. Tools may be very simple or sophisticated. Richness of tools is a combinational measurement of the quantity and quality of the tools. For example, among the tools for supporting the collaboration function, email communication is a simplest tool while the collaboration room (supporting both asynchronous and synchronous communications) is a much more sophisticated tool. When it is said that an IES has richer tools, it means the IES has relatively many and sophisticated tools to support a variety of functions. When developing or evaluating an IES, we must also consider the richness of tools provided by the system.

To cover the five educational organization scales, the integrated educational system, University21, has a framework that consists of several layers as shown in Figure 2. University21 is based on the technology and network layers. However, most of the software development effort has being put in the tool layer and the room layer. University21 provides a variety of toolkits in the tool layer for administration, course, collaboration, virtual instrument, database manipulation and system maintenance. Supported by the toolkits, different types of rooms can be constructed in the room layer. Currently, five types of rooms, virtual administration office (VAO), virtual private office (VPO), virtual courseroom (VCO), virtual collaboration room (VCR) and virtual laboratory (VLA) have been designed and developed. For the base scale of educational organization, i.e., an individual teacher, it may be enough to use only the virtual courseroom. For the small scale of educational organization, i.e., a group of teachers, it may be necessary to use several types of rooms, such as the virtual courseroom, the virtual collaboration room and the virtual laboratory. It is envisaged that an IES for a school or university should include many complicated administrative functions supported under a virtual administration office. Generally, tools in a smaller scale IES are a subset of tools in a larger scale IES.

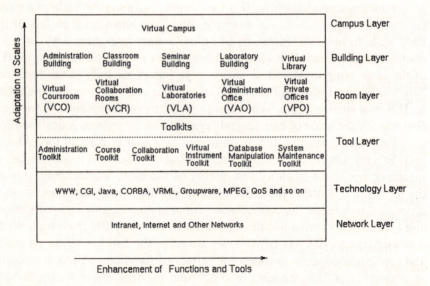

Figure 2   University21 framework for developing an integrated educational system

After clarifying what integrated educational systems are and designing the framework, it is necessary to give the fundamental criteria for developing an IES. For a successful integrated education system, the following criteria or features are essential.

Openness: The system should enable access and use from any types of computer platform with standard Web browsers (Netscape or Explorer) via the Internet. This will provide truly global teaching/learning with platform-independent applications.

Ease: The system should provide management and authoring tools with user-friendly interfaces, to make it easy for users to conduct teaching/learning activities.

Reliability: The system should enable recovery from emergent failures of computer systems or networks, and adaptation to network congestion and bandwidth changes.

Scalability: The system should be easily scaled from a smaller scale to a larger scale.

Extendibility: The system should be able to be continuously updated and extended with new functions and technologies developed.

Reconfigurability: Upon the framework of integrated educational systems, an IES can be developed to be a specified university or to be a general system which different universities can be derived from. As a general system, an IES should be reconfigurable for adaptation to special requirements and layouts of different universities.

University21 is such a general integrated educational system for all the defined scales of educational organization. It features rich tools, openness, ease of use, reliability, scalability, extendibility, and reconfigurability. A

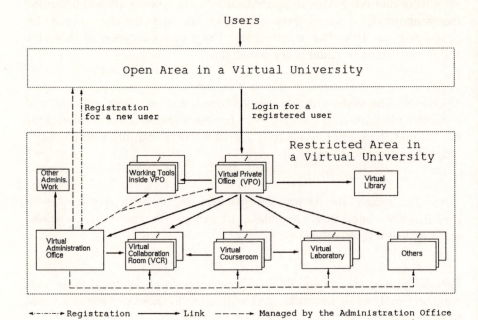

Figure 3 The general architecture of University21

general architecture of University21 shown in Figure 3 consists of two areas, the open area that is accessible by anybody and the restricted area that can be accessed by registered members only. The restricted area includes many virtual rooms associated with different activities in the virtual university. With considerations of the scalability criterion, each type of the rooms are implemented as relatively independent units such that they can be easily assembled or customized for building different scales and types of virtual universities.

Virtual Administration Office and Virtual Private Office

One of the main differences between a small scale of educational organization and a large scale of virtual university is that the latter usually requires more complicated administrative functions than the former. No matter what size of a virtual university, a virtual administration office is designated for managing users, curriculum, facilities, resources, plans, etc. The virtual administration office in University21 has been incorporated with the following functions:

user administration:
- to manage different users including staffs, teachers, students and visitors
- to manage user registration of joining the university, user quit for leaving the university, and student graduation
- to manage users' profile and statistics data.

curriculum administration:
- to manager the curriculum
- to handle teachers' requests of creating, changing or cancelling a course
- to deal with students' requests of selecting or withdrawing from a course
- to manage graduation research on proposing/selecting themes and selecting students/supervisors.

research administration:
- to handle (delete or add) research proposals
- to manage research group members
- to assign/remove/clean virtual collaboration rooms for each research group.

system administration:
- configuration
- maintenance
- resource allocation.

A private office is an individual work surface that is owned by an individual for managing personal activities and private data in a virtual university and entering other working rooms. To imitate individual office or desk space in a real university, the virtual private office enables users to work or study comfortably and efficiently and have the feeling of being immersed in the virtual university like a physical university. A virtual private office includes three sets of functions as shown in Figure 4(a). The first one is to manage personal activities and data, such as schedule, milestone, personal data, password, etc. The second one is to create a new online course by a teacher or select a course by a student. The last one is to provide mechanisms and hyperlinks for a user to enter other rooms.

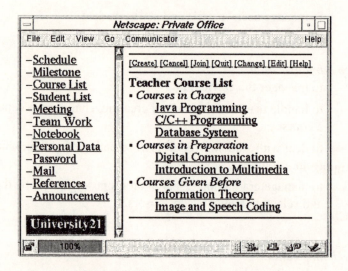

Figure 4a An example of the private office for a teacher

Management of personal activities and data is supported by a set of tools. For example, **Course List** is supported by course managers. There are two course managers. One is for teachers and the other is for students. When **Course List** in the left frame is clicked by a user, if the user is a teacher, the teacher course manager is automatically evoked; otherwise the student course manager is evoked. A course list related to the user will be shown in the right frame. The right frame in Figure 4(a) shows a teacher's course list. The courses on the list fall into three categories: *Courses in Charge, Courses in Preparation* and *Courses Given Before*. The teacher can create a new course by clicking **Create** or select a course to do some operations on it, such as cancelling, joining, quitting, changing or editing the course as shown in Figure 4(a). Figure 4(b) gives an example of a teacher creating a new course, Digital Signal Processing. After clicking **OK**, the course title, Digital Single Processing, will be listed under *Course in Preparation*. Then the teacher can enter the virtual courseroom of the course by clicking the course title to allow authoring and preparation of the course.

Figure 4b An example of creating a new course by a teacher

Virtual Classrooms

In a conventional university, a course is usually taught at a classroom. It, thus, seems natural to build a virtual classroom to provide an online course in a virtual university. However, a real classroom is often used for many courses in different periods while an online course should be always open so that students can access the course at any time upon their schedules and paces. It is, therefore, more rationale to use courseroom metaphor to represent a virtual environment, called virtual courseroom, for each online course. The virtual courseroom is incorporated with many software tools to systematically support for a teacher to author of online materials, organize teaching activities and instruct students, and for a student to access the online course and efficiently interact with a teacher and other students. University21 automatically assigns a virtual courseroom for each online course given or to be given. To be able to support a wide range of online courses with different content features and to foster a variety of teaching/learning styles for different teachers/students, the virtual courseroom has been designed and implemented based on a general and flexible architecture, called a hyper-environment. It consists of four parts: exploration environment, supplement environment, evaluation environment and collaboration environment as shown in Figure 5(a). The 'hyper' means that the courseroom can support a variety of teaching/learning activities and their efficient transitions. Figure 5(b) shows a web page of a developed virtual courseroom for the course, C Programming.

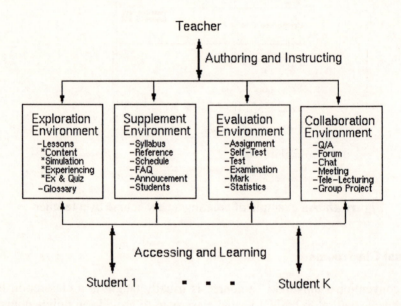

Figure 5a Hyper-environment architecture of the virtual courseroom

Exploration Environment

To master the contents of a course, students have to read a textbook, execute simulations, and conduct experiments and exercises. The ideal case is that students can explore different contents related to the course they are taking. The exploration environment helps teachers to efficiently prepare lesson contents, simulations, experiments and exercises, and enables students to effectively use those online materials.

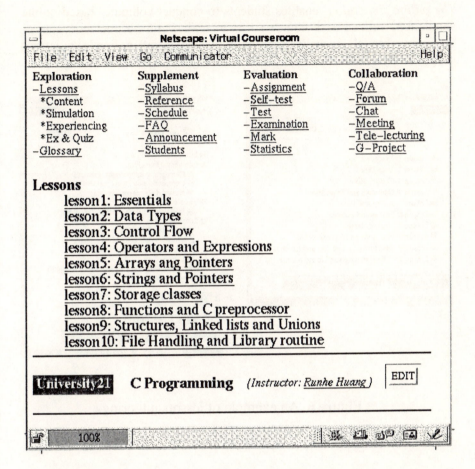

Figure 5b The WEB page of a virtual courseroom for C programming

The online content: the online material created by teachers and accessed by students via networks. When a courseroom is assigned to a course, there are no lessons and associated lesson contents in the courseroom at the beginning. A teacher may add lessons and edit lesson contents by using authoring tools in the courseroom as shown in Figure 6. Video and sound of recorded lecturing given by a teacher are available to provide lively explanations as shown in Figure 7.

The online simulation: enables students to conduct computer based online simulations related to a course so as to understand abstract concepts or formulae through visualization. Two examples of online simulations supported by virtual instrument tools will be given in Section 6.

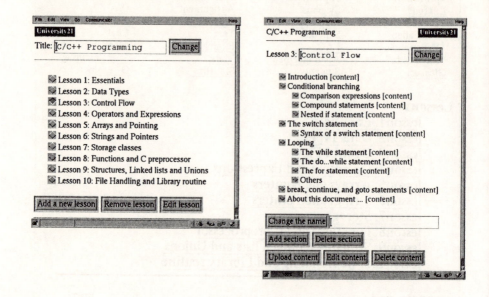

Figure 6 An example of lesson authoring

The online experiencing: allows students to be immersed in an environment synthesized by the virtual reality technology, and to experience what they have learned in order to deepen and widen their knowledge.

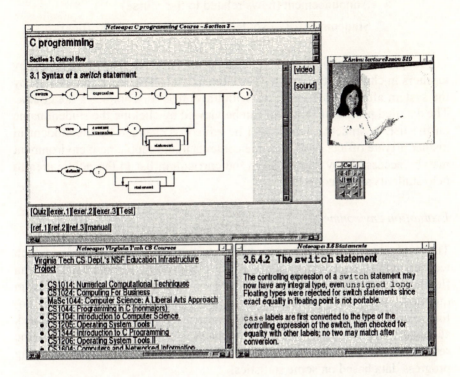

Figure 7 An example of a lesson with video, audio and online references

The online exercise and quiz: for students to digest and do self-check on what they have learned. These exercise and quiz problems are created by a teacher and closely related to associated lesson contents.

Supplement environment

To help student learning, some supplementary information or data related to a course is bonded together and placed in the supplement environment that includes:

- Syllabus
- Reference (links to other web pages or sites)
- Schedule (suggested schedule for learning the course)
- FAQ (frequent asked questions)

–   Announcement (news related to the course)
–   Students (a list of students with links to their profiles).

The supplementary information, except the student list, is updated by teachers in charge of the course. The student list is updated automatically by the system after a student selects, withdraws from or completes the course. The detailed profile of a student can be viewed by clicking the student name on the list. A student's profile can be edited or changed by the student in his/her private office. Further, some contents in the supplement environment may be accessible by anyone from the curriculum list in the public area to help students select courses.

Evaluation environment

The evaluation environment is an interactive environment under which teachers and students can conduct the following activities: (1) Teachers can flexibly create or modify on-line quizzes, on-line exercises or on-line exam questions. (2) Students can submit or participate in on-line quizzes or on-line exercises, and even take on-line tests easily. (3) A teacher can check students' assignments and tests automatically or manually and report the results to the students promptly. (4) Teachers can access students' learning progress data based on some statistics.

In University21, students' assignment and test data are well structured and stored in the main server. Teachers can easily retrieve the data. The tools for supporting the functions in this environment are classified in the following four sets:

authoring tools: for a teacher to create online assignments or online tests

execution tools: for a student to carry out online assignments or online tests

checking tools: for automatically checking and grading students' assignments

managing tools: for storing and retrieving assignment, test and student progress data.

Six types of questions are available in University21. They are (1) multiple choice quiz (MCQ), (2) **true** and **false** question (TFQ), (3) fill in the blank (FIB), (4) typing in answer (TIA), (5) programming from scratch (PFS), and (6) programming with skeleton (PWS). Figure 8 shows an example of a teacher creating different types of questions for an assignment of the course, C/C++ Programming. Figure 9 shows an example in which a teacher creates a PWS type of question, a student answers the question, and the solution is automatically checked.

With regard to on-line tests or exams, security for avoiding students' cheating is an important and challenging issue. In University21, the security for an online test is partially realized by using a unique full screen with one-time login control. When a student logs in to take a test, the test page will occupy the full screen of the monitor so as to make accesses of the other files and communications with others via networks impossible. After a student logs out the test, the student's next login to the same test is automatically refused by the system. So each student can only take a test once.

Collaboration environment

It is widely realized that teaching and learning can benefit much from a variety of collaborative activities. Collaborations among a group of remote people are generally classified into synchronous collaborations that refer to group joint work at the same time, and asynchronous collaborations that refer to group joint work at different time. Both the synchronous and asynchronous collaborations should be supported and the corresponding collaborative functions have been incorporated into the virtual courseroom. In University21, the functions for supporting the collaborative activities in the virtual courseroom are bonded together in the collaboration environment that includes:

- Q/A (email based questioning/answering, asynchronous),
- forum (newsgroup or bulletin based discussions, asynchronous),
- chat (text based real-time communications, synchronous),
- meeting (VCR based, synchronous),
- tele-lecturing (VCR based, synchronous),
- group project (VCR based, asynchronous and synchronous).

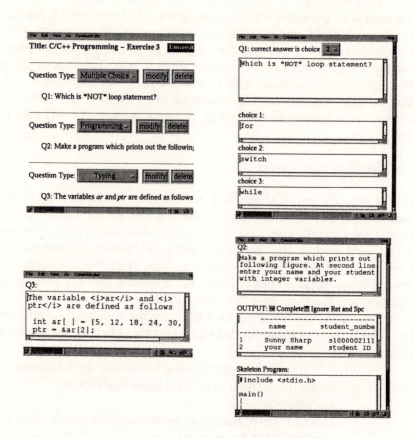

Figure 8 An example for a teacher to create different questions

The tele-lecturing function enables a teacher to give a lively lecture to remote students. It is synchronous communication and most information flows are from a teacher to students even if some information flows from students to the teacher are possible. This phenomenon is called asymmetric communication. The group project refers to a project that a group of students jointly work on. The project is conducted by a series of collaborative activities, such as discussions, meetings, implementation, and writing reports, and so on. Each group project, of course, is well prepared by a teacher to increase learning efficiency. Communications are both

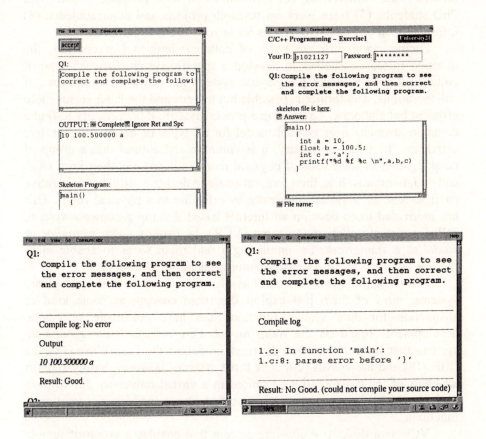

Figure 9 Authoring and automatic checking of a C/C++ program

asynchronous and synchronous. The meeting, tele-lecturing and group project are sophisticated teaching/learning collaborations that are based on an important component of University21, VCR (Virtual Collaboration Room), to be discussed in the next section.

Virtual Collaboration Rooms

In addition to a course oriented collaborative activities such as the meeting, tele-lecturing and group project, in a university, there are more types of group collaborative activities, such as, (1) non-course oriented meetings, seminars and conferences, (2) instructions of undergraduate, Master and PhD students, (3) team work on research projects and other subjects, (4) informal open-ended conversations for anyone to freely join, etc.

Facing many different types of collaborations in University21, the question raised is whether to develop a specific system for each type of collaboration or to develop a general system that can support all types of collaborations. The former is possible but tedious and the latter seems more efficient but elaborate. To develop a general system, it is necessary to find a common abstraction or general model for all types of group collaborative activities. In a real university, it is common and natural that a group of people gather in some kind of physical room and carry out their joint work and collaborations. It is, therefore, rationale to design a virtual collaborative environment for a virtual university by referring to a physical room. This has motivated us to develop an Internet based desktop groupware system, called a virtual collaboration room (VCR), by using a *room metaphor* or *model* as a framework, i.e. emulating a real room so as to enable more flexible and natural collaborations among teachers and students.

Although the word of room has also been used in other groupware systems, most of them just exploit the room concept as some kind of abstraction for their system functions and have not made systematic developments based on the room model. Few representative groupware systems that are truly based on the room model are the TeamWave [18], the CBE [19] and the worlds [20]. The three systems, however, hardly support all kinds of the collaborations required in a virtual university due to their limited object types, unnatural object features and weak awareness functions.

VCR is a desktop groupware system that enables a group of remote individuals to flexibly and naturally conduct their collaborative teaching/learning/working over the Internet. The flexibility refers to ability for people to use the VCR for a variety of collaborative activities without constraints on collaboration types, working styles, group scale, and system platforms. The naturalness refers to people feeling that their collaborations in the VCR are as natural as in a real room. As a general purpose collaboration room, the VCR can support a variety of group or team oriented activities. In fact, the VCR is customized to be a more concrete room related to a specific collaboration type, such as:

meeting room: for a group of people to hold a meeting, seminar and conference,

tele-lecturing room: for a teacher to give a lively lecture to remote students

project room: for students to participate in a course oriented group project

team room: for teachers and students to participate in a research oriented joint project

instruction room: for the supervision of undergraduate, master or PhD research

cafe room: for informal discussions or general chatting.

A collaboration room can be *group owned* or *common*. A group owned room is owned and managed by a specified group for its lifetime while a common room is used by different groups during different periods of time. A collaboration room can also be restricted or *open*. A restricted room allows only assigned users to enter while an open room is open to anyone until the predefined user limit is reached. For example, the meeting room and tele-lecturing room are common rooms, the project room, team room and instruction room are group owned rooms, the cafe room is an open room, and the team room and instruction room are restricted rooms.

A user may enter different VCRs from a courseroom to conduct an online course related tele-lecturing and group project, from a virtual private office to carry out student instruction and team work, or from a virtual administration office to have a staff meeting. A virtual university, therefore, has many rooms open simultaneously. For handling these rooms, the room administration related to each type of rooms is required. Two examples are given in Figure 10a and Figure 10b to show how a meeting room administration and a group project administration function. The meeting room administration can create many meeting rooms that are used by different groups of users for specified topics. The meeting room administration can schedule all events held in a meeting room. Similarly, a group project administration can create many group project rooms that are used by different groups to conduct the specified project.

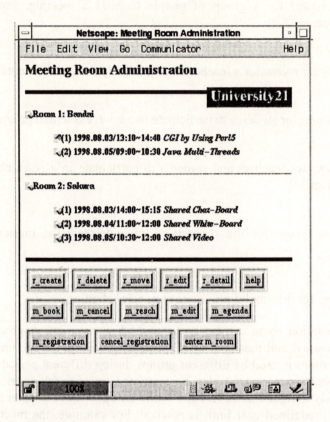

Figure 10a Meeting room administration

Since there are many rooms working simultaneously in University21, servers are constructed in a tree structure as shown in Figure 11. There are a number of room servers under the central server and a room server is responsible for activities associated with a collaboration room. The central server is run on the University21 main sever, and it holds data about all rooms, including a list of rooms, a list of members in each group, a list of room servers available on the campus network, data used by each of rooms, and so on. The central server receives discussion records from the room server, and stores data in the resource database of University21. Occasionally the central server sends a previous discussion record to a client who makes a request. During group collaboration, data received from a

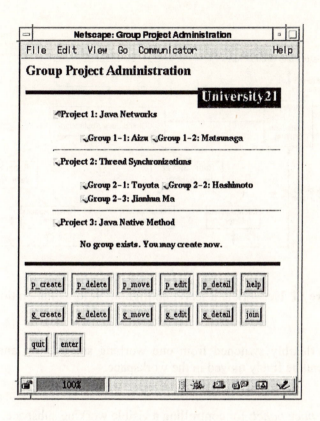

Figure 10b Group project administration

client is broadcast by the room server to other clients thus updating the shared group data.

A user can enter the VCR from any Java enabled Web browser. Figure 12 shows an example of a VCR layout. A VCR is divided into several regions and each of them has different functions as follows.

A workspace: a virtual space or a container where live objects are placed and users conduct work via interactions with the objects. Due to a limited size of the display window, the display window is regarded as a visible subspace of the workspace. The workspace in VCR is divided into six working subspaces and only one of them is visible at a time. However, it

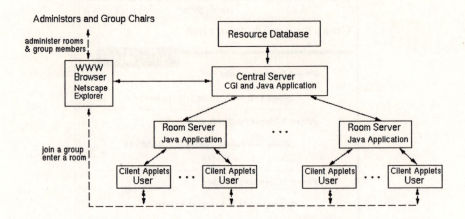

Figure 11 Network and server configuration for collaboration rooms

can be flexibly switched from one working subspace to another and an object can be freely moved in the workspace.

A workspace panel: for controlling a visible working subspace.

An object cabinet: is for storing and creating available objects. An object may be taken from the cabinet and put it in the workspace space.

An object panel: for controlling the objects in the workspace.

A user panel: for management of user's presence (enter, exit, temporarily leave or return to a room), and status (a chair, a presenter or regular members).

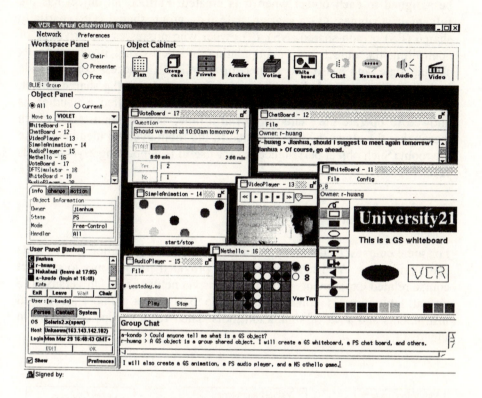

Figure 12 An example of room layout of the VCR

A group chat: a text-based chat shared by all group members. When someone would like to chat with only a subset of people, he/she can create a partially shared chat board.

To support many different collaborative activities, VCR facilitates a variety of objects including chat-board, whiteboard, planning, voting, applet for interactive simulations, plain text file, HTML file or web page, image, graphics, audio, video, animation and recorded object [21]. Each object has a life cycle from birth, alive to death. The birth of an object means that the object is created and put in a group workspace. Conversely, the death of an object means that it is destroyed and removed from the workspace. To distinguish different objects in the workspace, a unique ID number should be assigned to each object when it is created. Further, an object has the following attributes: (1) a sharing state, i.e., group shared (GS), partially shared (PS) or non-shared (NS), (2) owner who possesses the privilege of controlling the object, e.g., manipulating and destroying it, changing its sharing state, and passing its ownership to others, (3) access control mode including the free mode by which everyone can operate the shared object, and the rotation mode by which only one member, called a handler, is allowed to operate the shared object at a time, and (4) persistence which means that the object will be persisted in the room even all members leave the room (Such object persistence is very useful in supporting asynchronous collaborations).

Virtual Laboratories

For some courses, students are required to learn through online experiments and simulations. A virtual laboratory is provided for students to conduct course related experiments and simulations via networks. In University21, a virtual laboratory is constructed on the basis of a number of virtual instruments and a set of simulation tools. Their relationships are shown in Figure 13.

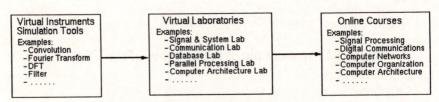

Figure 13 Relations among courses, virtual laboratories, and virtual instruments and simulation tools

After the completion of a curriculum in a virtual university, system managers in the university can construct a number of laboratories for those courses that require students to do online experiments or simulations. Consequently, the managers have to select associated virtual instruments and simulation tools for inclusion in a virtual laboratory. For example, the course Digital Signal Processing requires a Signal & System Laboratory for supporting students conducting some online simulations. The system managers may develop or select some software tools, such as, convolution,

Fourier transform, DFT (Discrete Fourier Transform), filters, and others to be included in the laboratory. Currently, various simulation tools are available on the market, but most of them are stand-alone applications. To be included in a virtual laboratory and used via networks, these stand-alone applications have to be modified to be computer platform independent applications. There are two approaches to achieve this.

The first approach is to place an application on the university servers and to run the application when a remote user makes a request. The user has a display surface at his/her terminal and can interact with the application through interfaces. To ease use, it is necessary to design user-friendly interfaces between users and the applications. WEB and CGI together may be used as a bridge. The drawback of this approach is that it seriously degrades the performance of the university servers with increasing number of users. Therefore, University21 does not take this approach.

The second approach is to place an application in the university server but to transfer the application to a user's local machine when the user makes a request. The application is run in the user's local machine. To do so, the application should be computer platform independent. JAVA applets are considered suitable for such applications. One important advantage of this approach is the reduction on the server's load. Therefore, University21 takes this approach and uses Java applets for developing virtual instruments or online simulations. When preparing an online course, a teacher can choose some virtual instruments and/or simulation tools for inclusion in associated lessons from a virtual laboratory. A hyper-link with necessary instructions in a lesson enables students to perform a corresponding simulation. An example of DFT simulation in the course, Digital Signal Processing, is shown in Figure 14. The simulation helps students to understand abstract concepts and formulae.

Collaborative experiments and simulations are also effective ways for students to learn a course. On the basis of Java technology, simulation tools and a general communication protocol in the collaboration room are developed. Conversion from a single-user simulation to multiple-users is aided by exploiting the Java delegation event model. Figure 15 shows an example of a simulation for multiple users.

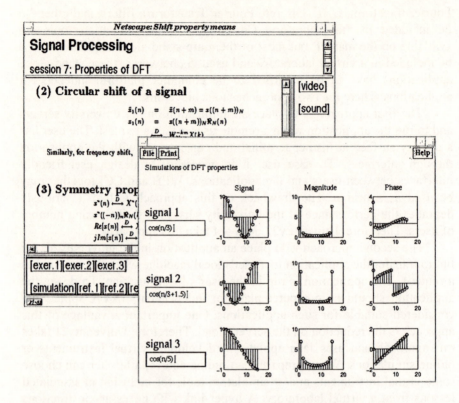

Figure 14 An example of DFT simulation in learning the Signal
Processing course

Conclusions and Future Work

Research and development on computer-supported teaching/learning over networks have been conducted for many years and most systems still support only teaching and learning of one or a few online courses. There are, however, more intertwined activities beyond just teaching and learning courses in schools and universities. It is an important research direction to develop a standard and unified integrated educational system for systematically supporting all activities in virtual schools and universities of the future. However, it is a very challenging task, in particular when an IES is designed for a large scale of educational organization. There are two difficulties: the lack of a clear definition and a general framework of the

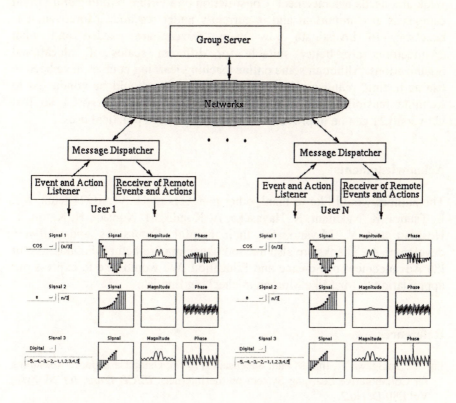

Figure 15 An example of Fourier transform simulation for
collaborative multiple users

IES, and the fact that an IES can not be built by just putting all available tools together. Therefore, our research began with clarifying the concept of the IES and designing a general IES framework. The IES framework proposed may be incomplete and needs further improvements. We believe that more work should be done on the fundamental issues so as to form some guidance for effectively developing and precisely evaluating IESs. The framework of University21 consists of several layers. The development of the toolkits at the tool layer has been done in a previous project, CHEER.

This chapter is mainly focused on the development at the room layer. Our work on developing the virtual office and the virtual laboratory is relatively weak and needs enhancement. Construction of a virtual building and virtual campus is also important and is currently under research. Moreover, it is necessary to investigate how many servers are needed and what architectures are better suitable for different scales of educational organizations. Although some online teaching/learning courses have been in use as testing, many more tests and experiments should be conducted to examine feasibility and evaluate performances of University21 so that University21 can be improved and enhanced through practical uses.

Acknowledgments

The authors would like to thank other members of University21 team, Mr. E. Tsuboi, K. Nakatani, R. Hayasaka, A. Kondo, M. Nonaka, H. Katou, T. Hoshino and Y. Miyano, for their helpful discussions and software developments. Thanks are also due to Fukushima Prefectural Foundation for the Advancement of Science and Education. We would like to express our appreciation to Mr Mike Morgan in checking English.

References

Fuji T., Tanigawa T., Inui M. and Saegusa:T. (1997); Using Case-Based Reasoning for Collaborative Learning System on the Internet, *IEICE Trans. Inf. & Syst.*, Vol.E80-D, No.2.

Giroux S. et al,(1996);: A Platform for Epiphyte Advisor Systems Dedicated to both Individual and Collaborative Learning, *Lecture Notes in Computer Science, Intelligent Tutoring Systems,* Volume 1086.

Greenberg S. and Roseman,M. (1998); Using a Room Metaphor to Ease Transitions in *Groupware. Research report 98/611/02*, Department of Computer Science, University of Calgary, Calgary, Alberta, Canada, January.

Hiltz S. T., (1995); The Virtual Classroom, Ablex Publishing Corporation.

Huang R. and Ma J. (1998) Designs of a Collaborative Teaching/learning Environment, *4th International Conference on Networking* Entities (*Neties 98*: Networking for the Millennium), pp46-49.

Kunii T. L., Ma J. and Huang R. (1997); Towards Direct Mapping between Information Worlds and Real Worlds, *The Lecture Notes in Computer Science, Visual Information Systems, Volume 1306* (1997).

LearningSpace, http://198.114.68.60/

Lee J., Prakash A. Jaeger T.and Wu G. (1996); Supporting Multi-user, Multi-Applet Workspaces in CBE, in the *proceeding of the ACM CSCW 96*, pp344-353, Cambridge, MA, November.

Ma J. and Huang R. (1996); Improving human interaction with a hyperworld, 1996 Pacific *Workshop on Distributed Multimedia Systems*, pp46-50, Hong Kong, June.

Ma J. and Huang R. (1998); A Natural Networked Computer based Integrated Teaching/Learning Hyper-environment, *The 1998 International Conference of the Learning Sciences*, Atlanta, Georgia.

Ma J., Nakatani R. and Huang R. (1996); Communications, Management and Manipulations of Objects in a Virtual Collaboration Room, *The 6th International Conference on Distributed Multimedia System*, Aizuwakamatsu, Japan (1999).

Ma J., Huang R. and Tsuboi E (1998); Cheer: a Computer-based Hyper-Environment for Educational Reformation, *Proc. Intl. Conf. on Computational Intelligence and Multimedia Application*, Australia.

Ma J., Huang R., Tsuboi E. and Hayasaka R. (1998); A Multimedia Collaborative Environment for Distant Education, *The Fifth Pacific Workshop on Distributed Multimedia Systems*, Taipei.

Mansfield et al. (1997); Evolving Orbit: A Progress Report on Building Locales, in the *Proceeding of the Group 97 International Conference*, pp.241-250, ACM Press.

Millan E. et al.:   GITE: Intelligent Generation of Tests, *Lecture Notes in Computer Science*, CALISCE 96, Volume 1108.

Roger N., Gilles G. and Claude F. (1996); CREAM-Tools: An Authoring Environment for Curriculum and Course Building in an Intelligent Tutoring System, *Lecture Notes in Computer Science, CALISCE 96*, Volume 1108.

Strack S. D. (1998); WebFace: an Architecture for Computer Mediated Communication, *Proc. Intl. Conf. on Computational Intelligence and Multimedia Applications*, Australia.

TopClass, http://www.wdtsystems.com/

Virtual-U, http://virtual-u.cs.sfu.ca

Web-CT, http://homebrew1.cs.ubc.ca/webct/

WCB, http://www.madduck.com/wcbinfo/wcb.html

8 Collaborative Virtual Environments for Problem Based Learning

JOZE RUGELJ
UNIVERSITY OF LJUBLJANA, SLOVENIA

Abstract

A common feature of problem-based learning (PBL) is to provide a range of resources that the students, working in groups on real-world problems, can access to obtain assistance with solving the problems. Typical characteristics of PBL suggest introduction of computer supported collaborative learning environment.

This chapter presents reference model for such environment, consisting of four groups of components used to support functions concerning access to different knowledge sources, external communication, communication in a group, and facilitation and compensation. Most important knowledge sources in the environment are virtual textbooks, prepared by teachers, and knowledge trees that grow as a result of collaboration between all users. The tools used for communication in a group and the tools for facilitation and compensation together form virtual classroom that can to great extent help its users to overcome the obstacles that appear due to spatial and/or temporal separation.

Virtual presence in virtual classroom can give participants the impression of a membership in a community. Facilitation tools are used to facilitate human thought, i.e. showing information in a way that makes solution more obvious than the original representation of the same information. In common educational settings facilitation was one of the main teacher's tasks, while in collaborative computer supported virtual environments he becomes more an advisor, a manger of learning space and organizer of the work rather than full-time direct provider of knowledge.

Introduction

Problem based learning is an instructional procedure that, in contrast to conventional education, transfers control over the learning process from the teacher to the students (Schmidt 1993). Students are encouraged to formulate and then follow their own learning objectives and to select the learning resources that best suit their information needs. The role of teachers is mainly in providing advice and suggestions for further work.

Several characteristics of the problem-based learning approach have been identified that are common to most problem-based learning courses (Boud 1991):

- As far as possible 'real-life' problems are used to engage the students in the learning process;

- Subject content often crosses the traditional subject boundaries;

- Students collaborate in small groups to develop a solution to the problem;

- The groups are assisted by a facilitator who is not necessarily an acknowledged expert in the content area that relates to the problem;

- Information on how to develop solutions to the problem is not usually given, although resources are available that assist in the process of approaching and solving the problem;

- Required areas of learning are identified by the students through their process of solving the problem and resources are available (either supplied or sought out by the students) to assist in these areas.

We found that most of the above-mentioned characteristics of problem-based learning suggest the introduction of a computer supported learning environment. Use of real life problems in learning process, interdisciplinarity and required high degree of self-dependence all benefit from access to the Internet, the richest information resource available today.

Collaborative learning is a key part of the Problem Based Learning (PBL) approach. A small group of students that meets weekly or even more frequently is faced with a problem to be solved. As students articulate and reflect upon their knowledge, learning and transfer are facilitated. PBL supports development of scientific understanding through real-world cases, development of reasoning strategies and development of self-directed and life-long learning strategies.

In most of the traditional educational settings organization of work of the above-mentioned working group is not an easy task due to various reasons. The problem is even worse in some specific cases, e.g. in enterprises where they are looking for an efficient way to organize various forms of life-long learning and training for their employees. Limited amount of time for group work and complicated scheduling procedures for meetings arrangement might prevent organizers of education from introducing innovative and effective approaches.

Computer-supported Collaborative Learning Environment

For these reasons we decided to suggest a reference model of a computer-supported collaborative learning environment that can be used to overcome many obstacles mentioned above by means of mechanisms for the support of group distributed in time and space. There can be different functionalities implemented in the learning environment. Harasim (1991, 1992) identified eleven functions of computer-supported collaborative learning environment that can efficiently support education in general. Rekkdal and Paulsen (Rekkedal 1989) prepared a similar list of functions with slightly different emphasis.

After careful examination of both lists we selected a subset of functions that are most significant for specific requirements of problem based learning environments for distributed working groups. According to a classification, introduced by McGrath and Hollingshead (McGrath 1994), the components of computer supported environment for collaboration can be divided into four groups where components in particular group are used to support functions concerning:

- access to external knowledge sources,
- external communication,
- communication in a group, and
- facilitation and compensation.

In the rest of the chapter we will present some most important characteristics and the role of particular group of components in the computer-supported collaborative learning environment.

Access to External Knowledge Sources

The first group of components consists of tools that are used to access different external information resources, needed by students in the process of problem solving. Some of these resources can be collected and structured in virtual textbooks, which represent a collection of specific learning materials, prepared for a particular subject of study or a particular course (Rugelj 1997).

As problem-based learning is interdisciplinary, students cannot find all the information they need in a single textbook; they need more freedom in information inquiry process. It is clear that the Internet with all its services for information retrieval can meet most needs.

On the other hand, too much freedom and abundance of information can provoke confusion and a feeling experienced by the students that they are lost in the cyberspace. At this point interventions from advisors or sometimes consultations in the group are needed. Skilful handling with the tools like searching machines and consistent requirement formulation are very important for effective work.

Virtual textbooks

The amount of information available on the Internet is enormous and it can be, for the time being, compared to the amount of information offered in printed media, but with much higher growth rate. Everybody could imagine the confusion of a student who is offered thousands of books, journals, and newspapers to study a certain topic.

To avoid confusion and to guide students while they are acquiring new knowledge, teachers and other experts have prepared printed textbooks where carefully selected knowledge is gathered and structured. We decided to implement a similar facility in the cyberspace where some locally produced "starting" learning materials would be extended and enriched with publicly available materials in the Internet. One of the powerful characteristics of the World-Wide-Web, the most promising telematics service in the Internet, is that it allows individuals to organize information resources from around the globe into new representations. We have implemented the concept of multimedia textbook consisting of WWW documents by means of knowledge trees.

Knowledge trees

A 'knowledge tree' is a list of pointers to applicable documents and can be built for each particular topic. We are using the term 'tree' here as the topic covered in the textbook can be further structured into subtopics and even more specialized units and thus we have a tree structure.

Knowledge trees are intended for a wide community interested in the selected subjects, i.e. teachers as well as students. They can both contribute their learning materials on a particular topic as well as the results of their explorations in the form of pointers to newly created documents or the documents, already existing somewhere in the Internet. Each entry in the knowledge tree is supposed to contain a short summary or a comment on the content and optionally short explanation about how each particular resource can be utilized.

Common Graphic Interface (CGI) forms are used as an efficient means for interactive integration of new information to knowledge trees that are publicly available as WWW pages. Edited knowledge trees represent appreciated high quality supplement to the existing learning materials.

Knowledge trees are simple databases that are growing as a result of long-term collaboration of users who are interested for particular subjects of instruction. Knowledge tree pages are public and are completely open for reading as well as for writing.

Access control mechanisms were a consideration and to prevent misuse we introduced a two-phase process for the construction of knowledge trees. In the first phase, anybody can contribute new items to the temporary tree opened for writing. In the second phase, the editor creates a read-only permanent tree from selected entries to the temporary tree and structures new contributions to appropriate branches of a tree. Thus, we can avoid presenting inadequate materials, but as both types of trees are public, users can permanently control editorial policy and can comment on it.

Proxy caching for efficient use of knowledge trees

Limited throughput of communication networks, especially of international connections, represents one of the most severe obstacles to efficient use of teleinformatics in education. As the network throughputs always lag behind throughputs needed by users and new applications, arriving services cannot be adequately supported by the existing infrastructure.

Congestions leading to unreasonable response times and unacceptable quality of service can discourage teachers and students from using telematics services. With the introduction of multimedia services data traffic increases exponentially and this additionally deteriorates working conditions.

The main expenditure in the international network connections is the high cost of leased lines offered by the national telecom company; the throughput is thus limited by the available funds. Fortunately, there are some other measures that can be taken to avoid such a difficult situation.

Before the WWW came into existence, users typically retrieved files by FTP. It had already been recognized that it placed an excessive load on networks, as well as on FTP servers, if each file were available in one place only, from which it would be retrieved by users all over the world. For this reason some mechanisms had been adopted for maintaining mirrors on sites distributed in suitable locations. However, it was the responsibility of the end user to identify and access the appropriate mirror.

Each WWW reference in its current form specifies reference to one particular host in the Internet. This means that without an appropriate mechanism, every WWW reference, no matter where it is from and no matter how often it is made, will make a network call to that specific site, leading to unnecessarily high use of network links and an excessive load on popular servers. In the long term, some location-free document reference is needed, together with the techniques for servers to co-operate to make mirrored copies of document available. This solution is global and is beyond our abilities. In the short term, different cache techniques can be applied with software solutions that are already available. We thus implemented an efficient mechanism for caching in our specific educational environment to overcome one of the local obstacles.

Most modern browsers now support some form of local caching where recently accessed documents are kept in the user's machine memory or on its disk. The user will, however, not benefit from the browsing (and fetching) of other WWW users. Caching is more effective on the proxy server than on each client. A proxy server is a server that serves as gateway between a local network and the outside world (Newman 1996). The proxy server allows various services, mainly caching of requests and a more secure means of obtaining documents. This saves disk space as only a single copy is cached. It also allows more efficient caching of documents that are often referenced by multiple clients, as the cache manager can predict which documents are worth caching for a long period and which are not.

A proxy cache is a way for a client to get remote pages via the server rather than direct from the original site. A WWW proxy cache acts on behalf of a number of Web browsing clients. Instead of clients having to fetch documents themselves, it makes a request to the proxy. The proxy fetches the document and returns it to the client. In addition the proxy keeps a copy of the document and if it is requested again by anybody from its domain, the proxy can satisfy that request without having to return to the remote site.

This is of greatest benefit when there are hundreds of clients all making use of the same proxy, as the chance that two clients will request the same document is greatly increased. This is especially topical in educational environments where inquiries are usually strongly correlated due to the specific organization of the work.

For distant documents the use of a proxy can give a much improved response to the user if the document is already in the cache; if the document is not in the cache than the response might be slightly impaired due to the participation of the proxy, although such differences are often masked by other network performance issues. For nearby documents, however, use of a proxy achieves no particular benefit and many clients can be configured with a list of domains from which they will retrieve documents directly, without using a proxy. Local domains should usually be put into this list.

We have now implemented a somewhat more elaborate set-up with two layers of cache proxy: a local proxy for one or more schools and a national educational proxy for Slovenia (Fig. 1.).

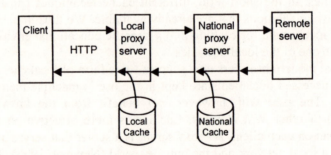

Figure 1 Two layers of caching

Clients would be configured to fetch local documents directly, while fetching all other documents via the local cache proxy. The local cache would be configured to fetch documents from anywhere in the country directly, whereas documents from abroad would be fetched via the national proxy cache. The national proxy, in turn, would serve documents from its cache when available, or fetch them from the ultimate server if necessary.

Virtual textbooks versus printed textbooks

Nowadays widely available technologies support multimedia representation of information and we can talk about multimedia virtual textbooks. They can be implemented in different ways. Very often they are stored on CDs, but they can also be stored on private servers, accessible via local network, or on public servers anywhere in the cyberspace. In this form they represent a substitute for traditional library.

Virtual textbooks implemented as knowledge trees in the WWW serve as a vehicle for more goal-oriented exploration and allow teachers and students to explore information space according to their abilities and according to their interests in particular topic. This type of personalization can be, to certain extent, implemented also in printed textbooks. But there are some advantages of WWW knowledge trees that are simply not feasible in printed textbooks.

Multimedia

One of the most important features of WWW and its supporting technologies is the ability to represent information in different media, such as video, sound, and high-resolution graphics as well as various synchronized combinations of them. These media can be much more attractive and efficient for information representation than conventional printed materials. As most of the browsers and supporting applications are available as freeware for educational purposes and no expensive hardware is required to run them, their use can also be justified by the price/performance ratio.

Real-time information delivery

Another important feature of WWW is its capability to deliver information just after it has been put on the server. In many cases information is interesting and useful only when it is available in real-time or with minimal delay. Weather forecasts, official quotations, market reports, or latest world news that can be used as supplementary learning materials have very short expiration terms.

Self-production

We have already mentioned that WWW is relatively simple to use. At the same time, it is not difficult for users to create their own WWW pages. The HTML language, which was developed for this purpose, is simple and there are a number of automatic translators that can translate different text formats, such as .doc, .rtf, .tex, or PostScript, to HTML. An efficient way of integrating new information to the existing documents is the use of CGI (Common Gateway Interface) forms. Users just type their text into appropriate forms and corresponding CGI software transfers the text to selected WWW page with adequate HTML elements. In this way, we have implemented the mechanism for interactive construction of knowledge trees, which is available to all users.

Collaboration

WWW is distributed and as such, together with the above-mentioned mechanisms for interactive document update, it can support different forms of collaboration between users (Bell 1995). In our case, users are secondary school teachers from all over the country as well as their students. Language barriers can represent a certain problem when we are trying to set up collaboration across the border.

External Communications

Whilst in the previous section we considered access to different information systems and databases, in this section we are concerned with communication with people who do not belong to a group of students and are not formally engaged in group activities as a tutor.

The most common communication pattern for external communication is one-to-one; i.e. a single member of a group communicates with an individual outside the group on behalf of the group or on his behalf. In this respect, external communication is very similar to the concepts for an access to the (external) information sources.

In problem-based learning environments this approach is mainly used to get some specific information from individual experts. Email is the most popular and the most convenient tool for this type of interaction.

Communication in a Group

This group of functionalities is certainly very important for the implementation of computer-supported collaborative learning environment. While the first two groups of functionalities are not very specific in comparison with individual work, i.e. we can use practically the same tools and mechanisms as for traditional individual learning and working, group activities require specific support. Characteristic communication patterns for collaboration in a group are one-to-many and many-to-many. It is well known that these patterns are not well supported as one-to-one communication pattern is prevailing.

Most important activities that need special support are:

- small group discussion and debating teams,
- learning partnership and dyads,
- peer counselling,
- team presentations (moderated by students),
- shared document repository,
- group authoring tools, and
- informal socializing.

We will consider the cases where members of a group for different reasons cannot meet face-to-face and most of work is carried out by means of the computer supported collaborative environment.

The first three activities in the list above (i.e. small group discussion and debating teams, learning partnership and dyads and peer counselling) can be successfully implemented in computer conferencing systems, which represent widely available collaboration tool for one-to-many and many-to-many communication patterns. In the cases where only two students are involved or when the discussion is not interesting for other members of a group, email can be used. If the students want to accelerate their work and they can participate in "a virtual group meeting", some synchronous tools for collaboration can be used. Internet Relay Chat (IRC) and similar tools (e.g. MUD) can be used for interaction. The problem is relatively low information throughput of these tools. Desktop multimedia conferencing tools, including video and audio, that allow much higher throughput, are becoming more and more popular and accessible for mass use.

In recent years the desktop computer has become the primary platform for creating and delivering multimedia applications that combine various materials - including text, sound, images and video. Multimedia involves the application of various communication channels to a communication exercise. In the simplest terms, desktop multimedia conferencing implies that a desktop computer is used to allow two or more people to communicate face to face using both video and audio as well as other shared multimedia resources such as text and images. Desktop video systems are targeted at both telecommunications networks such as ISDN and computer networks. There are a large number of products on the market, which meet different needs.

In 1992, a European project entitled Multimedia Integrated Conferencing for European Researchers (MICE) was launched (Handley 1993). The objective of the project was to provide all the technology components, other than the data network itself, to allow proper deployment of the tools for European multimedia collaboration in Europe. The MICE project relied heavily on developments, expertise and facilities provided in other national and international projects; only the international aspects, the technology integration, and the operational coordination were financed by the CEC. Therefore, the project used a range of existing conferencing equipment from other projects, which had a major bearing on the choice of subsystems used. The work of the MICE project that formally terminated at the end of 1995 continued as the project MERCI - Multimedia European Research Conferencing Integration. Different multimedia applications for communication support, such as audio and video desktop conferencing tools and shared whiteboard applications can be integrated into our working environment. These applications are mainly freeware and are available for different platforms (Unix, Linux, Windows95, ...)

Communication throughput requirements depend on information richness required by particular activities and play an important role in the design of a collaborative learning environment. In principle, communication channels represent a bottleneck for information exchange in any distributed system. Even the best tools for communication support can hardly deal with the amount of information that is adequate to performances of human sense organs. It is evident that the characteristics of communication channels between members of a group have a strong impact on the quality of collaborative work. It is not difficult to measure the throughput of a particular communications medium technically (e.g. in bits/sec), but there is no simple relation between the measured throughput and the efficiency of group work. Particular activities differ substantially as regards information richness. The richer is the particular task, the higher the throughput of communication channels required and the more efficiency degradation results from the throughput limitations.

Activities requiring groups to generate ideas tend to exhibit low 'richness'. They only require transmission of specific ideas; emotional and evaluative connotations about message and source are not required and are even considered to be a hindrance. Some problems involve situations where a single correct answer or preferred solution exists. Others concern situations that are uncertain or ambiguous when a given group or its members have limited information available about the situation at a given time, but that missing information could be obtained. Tasks of 'judgment' type are characteristic for situations that are equivocal, e.g. they can be viewed from more than one perspective and can be taken to have more than one meaning. It is obvious that these activities lie on the high richness end. Negotiations and conflicts resolving activities require transmission of maximally rich information, including not only facts, but also values, attitudes, affective messages, expectations, and commitments.

Team presentations require a synchronous approach to be effective. A shared whiteboard application, as a part of multimedia desktop conferencing systems, integrated into collaborative environment, is likely to be the best solution (Handley 1993). This allows controlled and synchronized presentation of text and different type of images. Together with audio and video channels it represents an environment that is really very close to traditional face-to-face meetings. An alternative is coordinated or guided presentation of WWW documents (Alton-Scheidl 1996).

Shared document repositories and **group authoring tools** can be implemented in many different ways. The knowledge tree, presented in the previous section as a tool for access to external knowledge sources, is at the same time a prototype of a shared document repository, used for specific model of indirect collaboration.

Recently, many advanced, generally applicable WWW based systems to support cooperation of distributed groups have been developed. The BSCW shared workspace (Appelt 1996), as the most popular representative of these systems is a document storage and retrieval system extended with features to support collaborative information sharing. A shared workspace can contain different kinds of information, such as documents, pictures, URL links, and threaded discussions. The BSCW server is an extension of a WWW server and the last version of the system is completely implemented by means of CGI scripts. This means that in principle any WWW server can be extended to become a BSCW server. Consequently, common WWW browsers can be used as BSCW clients. More details about the integration of WWW based systems for distributed group support into our learning environment can be found in Rugelj (1997a).

Since social communication is an essential component of education activity, online educational environments should provide opportunities for informal discourse. An online cafe as a metaphor for **informal socializing** can contribute to a sense of community among the users, forging a social bond that may offer motivational and cognitive benefits. It can be implemented by means of simple conferencing system, IRC or even desktop video-conferencing system.

Facilitation and Compensation

The activities from this group are intended to improve both speed and quality of group productivity. There are many functionalities needed in newly developed distributed environments, supported by different technologies for which no adequate tool has been developed and implemented. This is an area in which lack of interest in theoretical considerations has limited systematic development.

The tools that are used to support these aspects in the context of group-based learning can be classified into two main groups according to their roles: facilitation tools and compensation tools Hansen 1998). While the tools from the first group are designed mainly to facilitate human thought, the tools from the second group can, to a certain extent, compensate for difficulties that appear when collaboration is not face-to-face.

Facilitation tools

Facilitation tools can assist human thought through appropriate representation of data in a form that is easier to understand. The concept of facilitation is very close to Hutchins' idea of tools as "re-representations" (Hutchins 1990), that is, ways of showing the information that make the solution more obvious than it was in the previous ways of representing the same information. The classical example is the coordinate system invented by Descartes. Facilitation is proving easier with increasing processing power and multimedia I/O devices.

Compensation tools

Compensation tools are intended to help users in overcoming difficulties in communication and collaboration due to distribution of collaborating partners in time and space.

Pure compensation and pure facilitation tools represent two extremes. Compensation tools are supposed to be as transparent as possible, while facilitation tools, which can to a certain extent play the teacher's role, acquire their own identities. This classification can have some direct implications for the design of particular new tools, especially for the design of user interfaces, and for the ways in which new tools and existing tools are integrated into the working environment.

It is obvious that the boundaries between the two groups are not well defined and that there is a third group of tools in between that is growing fast, especially recently. The tools in this intermediate group are designed as facilitation tools but integrate facilities for communication and collaboration support. Typical simple examples are collaborative drawing tools and editors, whiteboards, and multi-user virtual environments. It is important that the tools from this last group are strongly embedded into the users' working environment, and that they do not represent an artificially implemented piece of technology.

Conclusion

The primary aim of this chapter has been to present a model of a computer-supported collaborative learning environment that is well suited to support problem based learning in groups, even when the members of a group are distributed in time and space. Students are encouraged to formulate and then follow their own learning objectives and to select resources that best suit their information needs. Teacher becomes more an advisor, a manger of learning space and organizer of the work rather than full-time direct provider of knowledge.

According to our reference model the components in the environment can be classified into four groups. The first group of tools is used to access knowledge sources that are needed by students in the process of problem solving. The most important knowledge sources in the environment are virtual textbooks, prepared by teachers, and knowledge trees that are constructed dynamically, as a result of collaboration of all users of the environment.

The second group of tools is needed for communication with experts, who are not directly present in the learning environment, but could contribute to the problem solving process. The tools from a third group are used for communication and information sharing in a group. They are used as 'ether' that allows information propagation from every single member of a group to all other members and therefore represent virtual classroom. Different telematic tools can be used to implement 'ether', depending on collaborative task to be carried out and its information throughput requirements. Virtual presence in the virtual classroom can give participants the impression of membership in a community and can thus substantially improve efficiency of learning.

Virtual classroom can be further improved by means of facilitation and compensation tools that represent the fourth group. Facilitation is used to 'facilitate human thought', i.e. for showing information in a way that makes solution more obvious than the original representation of the same information. Compensation tools are intended to help users in overcoming difficulties in communication and collaboration due to distribution of collaborating partners in time and space.

References

Alton-Scheidl, R.(1996): Web4Groups, *Proc. ERCIM workshop on CSCW and the Web*, Sankt Augustin, Germany.

Appelt, W., Busbach, U.(1996): The BSCW System: A WWW based Application to Support Cooperation of Distributed Groups, *In Proc. of WET ICE 96: Collaborating on the Internet*, Stanford University, 19.-21. June, 1996, Los Alamitos: IEEE Computer Society Press, pp. 304-310.

Bell, P., Davis, E.A., Linn, M.C.(1995): The Knowledge Integration Environment: Theory and Design, *Proc. Int. Conf. on Computer Support for Collaborative Learning, (CSCL 95)*, Bloomington, Indiana.

Boud, D. and Feletti, G. (eds.) *The challenge of problem-based learning*.

Handley, M.J., Kirstein, P.T., Sasse, M.A.(1993): Multimedia Integrated Conferencing for European Researchers (MICE*), Proc. JENC 93*.

Hansen, T., Dirckinck-Holmfeld, L., Lewis, R. and Rugelj, J. (1998): Using telematics for collaborative knowledge construction. In Dillenbourg, P. (ed.), *Collaborative Learning: Cognitive and Computational Approaches*, Pergamon - Elsevier Science.

Harasim, L.(1991): Teaching by computer conferencing. In Applications of Computer Conferencing to Teacher Education and Human Resource Development, ed. A. J. Miller, 25-33. *Proceedings from an International Symposium on Computer Conferencing at the Ohio State University*, June 13-15.

Harasim, L.(1992): Foreword. In *From Bulletin Boards to Electronic Universities: Distance Education, Computer-Mediated Communication, and Online Education*, M. F. Paulsen edt., University Park, Pennsylvania: The American Center for the Study of Distance Education.

Hutchins, E. (1990): The technology of team navigation. In Galegher, J, Kraut, R.E., and Egido, C. (eds.), *Intellectual Teamwork: Social and Technological Foundations of Cooperative Work*, Lawrence Erlbaum Associates, 1990, pp.191-220.

McGrath, J.E. Hollingshead, A.B.(1994): *Groups interacting with technology*, Sage Publications, Thousand Oaks.

Newman, D. R.; Johnson, C.; Webb, B.; Cochrane, C.(1996): An Experiment in Group Learning Technology. *Interpersonal Computing and Technology*, 4(1), September 1996, pp. 57-74.

Rekkedal, T., Paulsen, M.F.(1989): Computer conferencing in distance education: status and trends. *European Journal of Education* 24(1), pp. 61-72, 1989.

Rugelj, J.(1997): Computer Supported Network Based Learning Environment for the Workplace, *Proc. 3rd Int. Conf. on Network Entities*, Ancona, pp. TT3.1-3.4.

Rugelj, J., Svigelj, V(1997).: Computer Supported Multimedia Environment for the Support of Long-Distance Collaboration in Medicine, *In Proc. Symp. on*

Computer Based Medical Systems, IEEE Computer Society Press, Los Alamitos, California, pp. 215-220.

Schmidt, H.G.(1993): Foundations of problem-based learning: some explanatory notes, *Medical Education*, 27, pp. 422-432.

9 Factors Affecting Active Participation in a CMC Created for Distance Learners

TINA WILSON AND DENISE WHITELOCK
OPEN UNIVERSITY, UK

Abstract

Educational establishments in the United Kingdom are interested in understanding how Computer Mediated Communication (CMC), can be used to enhance student study, particularly on distance learning courses. Important issues related to this research are how it can be used to assist with difficult areas in the course material, during periods of intense study and how levels of participation can be sustained. This chapter discusses how a CMC environment afforded a support structure for students to discuss difficult areas of their course and engage in social interaction. We also investigate levels of participation, non-participation and the outside influences affecting involvement in the CMC. The findings of this study suggest that through the CMC, students could overcome certain difficulties with the course content and this abstract

Educational establishments in the United Kingdom are interested in understanding how Computer Mediated Communication (CMC), can be used to enhance student study, particularly on distance learning courses. Important issues related to this research are how it can be used to assist with difficult areas in the course material, during periods of intense study and how levels of participation can be sustained. This chapter discusses how a CMC environment afforded a support structure for students to discuss difficult areas of their course and engage in social interaction. We also investigate levels of participation, non-participation and the outside influences affecting involvement in the CMC. The findings of this study suggest that through the CMC, students could overcome certain difficulties with the course content and this infers that CMC promises to play an active role in the future of distance education.

Introduction

Institutions in the United Kingdom seeking to diversify into distance learning are keen to adopt Computer Mediated Communication (CMC) to improve course delivery and facilitate collaborative learning through simulation of face-to-face meetings. They want to understand how best to integrate CMC into their courses. The Open University has taken teaching on-line to home based students very seriously and has found that the perceived benefits include: sharing of experience, knowledge and expertise; being a member of a community; having reassurance and support; facilitating on-line self help groups; and a feeling of using a modern medium, see Wilson and Whitelock (1997a). As a result of many pilot projects making successful use of CMC see Mason, (1989), Alexander, and Mason (1994), this method of on-line teaching has been adopted wholeheartedly by course teams at the Open University. In 1998 this meant that at least 33,000 users (supported by our Academic Computing Service) were registered on the First Class conferencing system. Some 1,500 of these users were tutors who were engaged in course related activities with approximately 25,000 students. The remainder of users were students without a course specific requirement, who still wanted to make use of the conferencing system.

The introduction of CMC to course presentation raises the expectations of those involved whether they are the course providers, tutors or students. This chapter reports on how a CMC environment transformed the typical Open University students' practice of study. The emphasis is on longitudinal data with respect to student ease or difficulty with their computer science course and investigates how they made use of the CMC environment to support their course work. This discussion not only emphasises the students' levels of participation and non-participation but also more importantly reports on outside factors that influenced their involvement in the CMC environment. In fact ensuring good levels of student participation in CMC environments still remains an issue. Although levels of participation have been discussed in the literature, there is little mention about why students used the system less than expected and why a percentage stopped using the facilities altogether.

Before CMC could be adopted on a large scale at the Open University, projects investigated best practice in how to proceed. One of the projects which has helped to influence current usage was M205 - STILE ('Students' and Teachers' Integrated Learning Environment') see Mason (1996). This project included four universities in the United Kingdom. The Open University's implementation used a CMC environment (in addition to the

World Wide Web) with one hundred and ten students and nine tutors nationwide and in Europe over a period of ten months in 1995. The course catered for both technical and non-technical students. Our subjects ranged from novices through to experts in the use of CMC. This analysis of the M205 - STILE project highlights the problem areas on the course and indicates whether the students found that CMC provided a source of help with these problems and hence encouraged them to stay on the course. Indeed CMC provided a new form of communication between students and tutors and we discuss how they adapted to it and took advantage of this new medium. We also discuss how the system was useful when a study period became very intense such as before the exam.

We report on the students' willingness to take part in the M205 - STILE project and also discuss what factors prevented some students from participating more. Indeed the issues of sustaining participation have been reported, by Mason (1989) and reiterated by Mason (1994). She found that 'students' use of CMC ranged widely from total non-use, to minimal use, to more than the course requirements through to exceptionally heavy use'. There is little mention in the research about why some students used the system less than expected. However Grint (1989) alludes to some of the issues in a study involving twelve students. This further analysis of the M205 - STILE project takes up these issues with a larger body of students, firstly, by analysing what outside influences affected student participation in the CMC environment, and secondly, by investigating why some students used the on-line facilities less than expected.

Results

In order to assess how the CMC environment changed students work patterns and whether it was a tool that afforded pedagogical benefits, a range of empirical measures were collected. These were taken in order to understand:

- Problem areas during the course and whether CMC alleviated these difficulties,
- How students took advantage of this new form of communication,
- How CMC helped during periods of intense study and
- Factors affecting participation.

In order to collect relevant data pertinent to the above three issues, four questionnaires were sent out on-line to the students at staged intervals throughout the course. Questions from three of these four questionnaires are analysed here. The first questionnaire was sent out on-line two months after the course start date. Of the 94 students still on-line, 66% responded. The second questionnaire was sent out on-line after six months, to the 58 students who were still using the system. Of these 84% responded. A questionnaire sent out on-line just before the end of the course (after nine months) to the 58 students who were still on-line, received a response rate of 83%. To ascertain feedback from students who were no longer using the on-line system, we sent out a separate questionnaire by Royal Mail. This latter questionnaire probed these students about their reasons for using the on-line facilities less than expected.

Active Participation

Although many early on-line messages were from students looking for friends, there were periods in the presentation when students were not available. Indeed one student, who was able to make her presence felt, in that she had regular contacts, was concerned when feedback seemed limited. She said:

- A sudden silence from a normally regular contact.

- Are they OK? Have they broken down? Given-up? Maybe I should have put in a :)!!!!!

She expressed how much she depended on on-line feedback and her excitement when a new message arrived:

- Ooh! A flag in my Mailbox.

This would suggest the importance of a sense of presence and the need to be presenting to an audience. Even when a student is familiar and confident in the environment, participation is dependent on others not just the individuals input. Indeed Kraut, et al (1992) argue that 'in an electronic forum, where interactivity is reduced, achieving and maintaining momentum is difficult because of delays and uncertainties about when and if a message was delivered'. We could surmise therefore, that students less confident with the system could require more help and encouragement. Indeed CMC has been acknowledged as having both benefits and problems. Wegerif (1995) discusses the importance of 'establishing and maintaining a community' to encourage participation. Kraut, et al (1992) stress the importance of interactivity and feedback. Mason (1994) discusses one of the issues that makes it difficult to keep a cohesive on-line group. In her case she cited students who though not technical were very literate. She stated that 'in dynamic conferences, the keenest students jump in straight away, often with very competent or literate responses. Less confident students, or those who are not able to log on frequently, find that the discussion has always moved on or others have already made their point'. Acknowledging these difficulties, the M205 - STILE environment was set up to alleviate these problems by the introduction of an Interactive Media Facilitator or IMF, see Wilson and Whitelock (1996) and (1997b).

Problem Areas During the Course and Whether CMC Alleviated these Difficulties

The FirstClass conferencing system was selected to minimise any technical difficulties that students would encounter so that they could concentrate on using the medium to solve problems with their course work. Therefore we could ask the students about the types of problems they encountered as they proceeded through their computer science course. Not surprisingly the majority of students did not hit any problems at the start of the course, with 60% reporting that they found the course easy, see table 1. In fact students at this point were busy socialising on-line with their peers, as reported by Wilson and Whitelock (1996). As we would expect, however, their perception of problems on the course changed as they proceeded through the material. After six months 67% of the students reported finding the course moderately difficult while only 20% described it as easy, see table 1. Similar responses to the latter were received when we asked the same question nearer the end of the course. Looking at students difficulty with the course, we had an unexpected result with less students reporting difficulties midway and at the end of the course as compared to the beginning, see table 1. In fact the percentage finding difficulties with the course dropped from 18% at the start of the course to 12.5% at the end. It could be that the students found that the CMC environment supported their study and were able to make more use of it as they proceeded through the course. Indeed, students have stated that they would have abandoned the course if M205 - STILE had not been available. For example one student said "I think I might well have stopped if I had not had the support from M205 - STILE!"

	At the start of the course	After 6 six months	Near the exam
Course was easy	37	10	10
Course was moderate	13	33	31
Course was difficult	11	6	6
Didn't answer question	1	0	1

Table 1 Problem areas on the computer science course

Prior to the M205 - STILE presentation of the course, students had had to rely on either the telephone or Royal mail to describe their programming problems. With M205 - STILE they felt they could see electronically whether other students were experiencing the same difficulties as themselves. As one student put it M205-STILE added another dimension to this course, creating a bit of feedback as to how other students are doing'.

How Students Took Advantage of this New Form of Communication

The M205 - STILE environment enabled tutors and students to avail themselves of electronic communication. Therefore it might be expected that students would use their on-line tutorial to ask their tutor for help. Approximately 1/3 (27%) of the students who responded confirmed that they had asked their tutor for help in their tutorial conference. What perhaps is more interesting is the fact that 72% of the students did not feel the need to contact their tutor for help. Perhaps this is related to how easy or difficult they were finding the course. Certainly three quarters of the students who found the course easy did not contact their tutor. But what is surprising is that more of those students who were finding the course moderate to difficult did not contact their tutor for help either, see table 2. More students asked their peers for help rather than their tutor. When asked, a higher proportion of students rated their on-line interactions with their tutors as more important than with other students. However when they were asked who had helped them more with their learning a higher proportion reported other students rather than their tutor, see Wilson and Whitelock (1998a). Although they gave more status to the feedback they received from their tutors where they were looking for approval, they did not want to expose their lack of knowledge to the tutor but only to their peers. This was a new development in communication for Open University students who could normally only quiz each other at face-to-face tutorials or self-help groups which not all students attend.

	Asked tutor for help on-line	Did not ask tutor for help
Course was easy	9	28
Course was moderate	5	8
Course was difficult	2	9

Table 2 Students who asked their tutor for help

The fact that more of the students who found the course moderate to difficult did not ask their tutor for help is an interesting finding. They may have been afraid of appearing foolish in front of their peers. Personal email to their tutor may have worked better if this was the case. Perhaps they felt that they could not describe their difficulty in this medium. These students had not met each other nor their tutor before using the on-line environment and therefore their tutor may have seemed less approachable than in a face-to-face situation. If this was the case it would have been difficult to build up a rapport with their tutor. One wonders in fact if these students would have raised their query in a face-to-face session either but the specification of their problem using the textual nature of the CMC may have proved too difficult for them. Although the students' opinions differed about whether they should contact their tutor or their peers for help, they were still able to use the environment to communicate. What is more important is that they did communicate and solved problems through the medium with the people they felt most comfortable with.

How CMC Helped During Intense Periods of Study

The vast majority of students responded that they were interested in using the M205 - STILE environment for their revision, see Figure 1. If we take the categories five, four, and three together, we find that 67% of the students who responded anticipated using M205 - STILE for their revision. This is a high percentage of students considering that no extra material pertinent to revision was supplied. This suggests that the students felt that the environment itself created an atmosphere where they were able to revise with their peers, seek help from their tutor and use the search facility to locate messages relevant to their revision. In fact seventeen students representing 15% of the total students involved in the project left M205 - STILE for varying lengths of time during the year, but returned to use the system at a later date. Six of these students representing 5% who left the system in March and April, came back on-line in the period August to October 1995 when their exam was approaching, see Wilson and Whitelock (1998b).

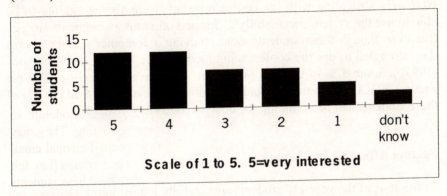

Figure 1 Student interest in using M205 - STILE for their revision

One student who did not answer this question made the comment that because they were in the Royal Navy they were not able to avail themselves of M205 - STILE to help with their revision. This comment of a lack of time was echoed by another student who rated the use of M205 - STILE for revision at '2'. This is not surprising since the use of the on-line system was in addition to the normal presentation of the course. A third student in this category commented that he was 'not really interested' because he liked to do his 'own thing for revision'. He did suggest however that 'a list of suggested revision topics would be useful' in the M205 - STILE environment.

When we analysed how students rated the CMC environment to solve their revision problems we found that for students in the moderate range with categories five and four taken together, 61 % anticipated that M205 - STILE would help with their revision, see table 3.

	Five	Four	Three	Two	One	didn't answer
Course was easy	2	1	1	2	3	1
Course was moderate	9	10	6	5	1	0
Course was difficult	1	2	0	1	1	1

Table 3 Students' rating of the CMC for revision against course problem areas

However when looking at the spread of responses between five and one, in the easy and difficult categories of table 3, it was obvious that the students appeared indecisive about how M205 - STILE would help with their revision. Students' difficulties with the course and ability to cope with the added technology are echoed by some of the tutors who said that those who were struggling with the course material 'were also struggling to be able to use the system successfully'. This and other tutor comments suggest that even though these students were studying a computer science course they struggled to use the conferencing medium, see Wilson and Whitelock (1997b). Some 67% of students (see figure 1) however had reported that the M205 - STILE environment could facilitate their revision and all but 2% of these students had been finding the course moderately difficult.

Factors Affecting Participation

At the start of the year 110 students successfully logged into FirstClass, our aim had been to have 100 students on-line. As would be expected, student usage of M205 - STILE did drop with time. However, students who left the system did not leave in droves but gradually trickled away. On average seven students left the system per month but 53% of the student participants were still on-line in September 1995, before their exam, see Wilson and Whitelock (1998b).

Many students continued to use M205 - STILE throughout their course. As mentioned earlier, (in the section 'how CMC helped during intense periods of study'), a number of students left the M205 - STILE system but returned later to use it for their revision. However a group of 35 students that is 32% of the participants reached a point in the year when they stopped using M205 - STILE altogether. It is often a complaint of educationalists that students do not make enough use of conferencing systems. Our findings when reviewed over the ten month period support the work of Mason (1989) and (1994) and Murphy (1994). Indeed Mason (1994) consistently found approximately 'one third of students using the system actively to put in messages; about one third reading messages and one third taking little or no part in its use'. Murphy (1994) echoes this point and reported that 'fewer than one third of the individuals in the survey account for nearly 80% of the reported CMC use, and another 20% indicate they do not use the medium at all, its availability not withstanding'.

Although our results concerning students who stopped using the on-line facilities were similar to those of other researchers, the question still remained about why students stop using the CMC facilities. To investigate this issue further, we asked the 35 (or 32%) of students who stopped using M205 - STILE, if the environment had not been as helpful as they had

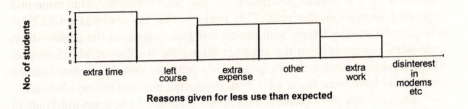

Figure 2 Students who used M205 - STILE less than expected

originally hoped. This questionnaire was sent out to these students by surface mail at the end of the course. We had a response of 74%. Students were asked to choose one or more of the following statements that best described their reason for using M205 - STILE less than they had originally intended because:

- it involved extra work
- it involved extra expense
- it involved extra time over and above normal course work
- they left the M205 course
- using a modem and email etc was not of interest
- other reason.

The highest rating suggested by these students, which affected their participation, was the extra time required to take part. One student commented that the course was more time consuming than they had expected and this had a bearing on their involvement. Another student echoed this point saying *I was keeping up with my M205 work... so had no time to spend browsing through the varied information available on M205 - STILE.* This issue of a lack of time is echoed by the majority of students who were still on-line rated a lack of spare time as the main reason for not participating more in M205 - STILE. This is not surprising since the M205 course itself has a high workload and the conferencing element was an add-on. The tutors also mentioned their own and their students lack of spare time, as discussed in Wilson and Whitelock (1997b). Although it seems that a high proportion of the students stopped using M205 - STILE because they left the course, the drop out rate was in line with the conventional presentation of the course. Of the students involved in the M205 - STILE project, 81% remained registered for the whole course. This corresponds with 83% of the whole population of the M205 course, who remained registered throughout the year. This suggests that the students on M205 - STILE were equally happy with the on-line presentation of the course when they were compared with the students taking the traditional M205 course. These retention rates are very good. This suggests that those who left the course may have been those who were struggling with the course material.

The students were given an indication in advance about on-line costs in their documentation. However, the extra expense in taking part was cited by some students as a reason for their lack of participation. So also was not knowing if the expense of the telephone bill was high or low since there was no indication of how long you were on-line and how many units you were consuming while on-line. Another student felt that this could be a very useful tool if it were faster as too much time was spent (and money) on-line before one could reach the bit of information which one required. Although some students did stop using M205 - STILE and some used it less than they originally intended, they were still keen on using this type of technology to help their learning and one commented she would be happy to be involved again next year. Another of these students said he found M205 - STILE quite useful.

It was interesting that none of the students chose the option showing disinterest in modems and email. This suggests that using the technology itself was quite straightforward. Indeed one student from the 'Other' category mentioned that on the whole she found the system to be quite easy to use. Only one of these students reported technical difficulties, and this was trying something that was not required. Therefore it was not surprising that he 'could not configure it to work correctly using the Beta release version of Win 95'. Some students in the 'Other category said it was difficult to participate more, because of: work commitments, pressure to find work, and looking at a VDU for extra information was too much.

One student who stopped using M205 - STILE after some time made the following very telling remark in a questionnaire. We were asking why she had stopped using the system. She said she thought that M205 - STILE was potentially very useful. Perhaps it was hijacked quite early on by a small group of users which put less experienced modem/pc users off? This suggests that the enthusiasm of some very technical students was perceived as taking the lead or taking over this environment. This student's comment needs further research to find out whether other students felt similarly. Mason (1994) mentions this finding, saying that although conferencing allows 'people who would normally be disenfranchised, to express their opinions...a small group can dominate the interaction...just as in face to face meetings'.

Summary

M205 - STILE afforded a support structure for students to discuss their course work and engage in social interaction. Difficulties with the course materials were reported by 18% of the students, just two months into the course. However this percentage reduced to 12.5% reporting difficult problems to solve with their course materials, both six and also nine months into the course, when they would have been more familiar with the use of the on-line system. There could be a number of reasons for this. For example some of these students may have left the course, but Wilson and Whitelock (1998c) reported that retention rates on the M205 - STILE version of the course were almost identical to those for the traditional version of the course. This does raise a question though, about why some students did not use the system as much as expected. Indeed some students reported that M205 - STILE helped them to remain on the course. Although smaller numbers of students contacted their tutor than might be expected particularly in the group experiencing the most difficulties, students were using the on-line facilities to socialise and also ask their peers for help rather than their tutor in some cases.

In addition to their lack of spare time, the extra expense in telephone bills was also an important factor to this group of students and influenced their level of participation. In order to allow students time to take part and fit participation around their already busy lives, the use of CMC needs to be more integral to the course. Students also need to be provided with tools such as an off-line reader to reduce their telephone bills.

The number of students who stopped using M205 -STILE (32%) complemented the findings of Mason (1989) and (1994), and Murphy (1994). However this chapter has also established some of the reasons why some students reached a point were they stopped using the on-line facilities altogether. Our findings based on a larger body of students than Grint (1989) suggest that there are issues related to a student's personal circumstances which can affect their level of participation rather than the adoption of the technology itself.

Conclusions

There is a critical period in which students need to get on-line in the first instance, otherwise they probably will not participate; we would suggest that the critical period is the first three weeks. An important issue for the students themselves is their lack of spare time that meant they used the system less than they would have liked. This is a time consuming activity, and the fact that some students stopped using the CMC facilities suggests that they were not convinced of its benefits for their learning. It must be borne in mind though that these students were using CMC in addition to their usual course load and therefore a lack of spare time is not too surprising. Both students who remained on-line and those who stopped using M205 - STILE mentioned this lack of spare time as being the main influence on their participation level. Indeed Newman and Newman (1993) found in one of their case studies that 'organizational interests' and 'time pressure' were strong influences. The students who stayed on-line throughout the year and this was a high percentage (see Wilson & Whitelock, 1998c), perceived themselves as not satisfied with their level of participation and would have liked to have participated more. This group also cited work commitments as a factor affecting their participation.

The M205 - STILE environment was constructed to facilitate student interaction in three different dimensions; these were the social, motivational and knowledge dimensions. Students did report using the environment in ways that can be accounted for, by this three dimensional system of analysis. For example students were very keen to use the on-line facilities to communicate with their peers and their tutor, they also anticipated using the system to help with their revision. The design of the M205 - STILE environment provided a flexible system into which students could dip into and out of at times suitable to them. They could use M205 - STILE when it facilitated their course work. It was better than the telephone and Royal Mail to describe program code. Also some students who had stopped using the system earlier in the year were able to go back on-line in time to revise for their exam. The CMC sustained and motivated students who would otherwise have been studying alone, through its facilitation of social contact. Students were able to use the on-line environment to overcome certain difficulties with the course content therefore it could be said that CMC offers the promise of playing an active role in the future of distance education.

Acknowledgements

We would like to thank all nine tutors involved in M205 - STILE. The research described in this chapter was undertaken in the Computing Department, Faculty of Mathematics and Computing, at the Open University as part of the STILE project. The project was supported by a grant from the Teaching and Learning Technology Programme that is jointly funded by the four higher education funding bodies, HEFCE, HEFCW, SHEFC and DENI.

References

Alexander, Gary and Mason Robin (1994). Innovating at the OU: Resource-Based Collaborative Learning Online. *Open University CITE Report, paper No 195.*

Grint, Keith (1989). Accounting for failure: Participation and non-participation in CMC. In Eds Mason, Robin & Kaye, Anthony, *Mindweave*, Pergamon Press, Oxford.

Kraut, Robert, Galegher, Jolene, Fish, Robert and Chalfonte, Barbara (1992). Task Requirements and Media Choice in Collaborative Writin'. In Eds Kraut, Robert, *Human Computer Interaction*, Volume 7. Lawrence Erlbaum Associates, Inc.

Mason, Robin (1989). Use of CoSy on DT200, 1989. *Internal Open University CITE Report,* Paper No. 99.

Mason, Robin (1989). An evaluation of CoSy at the Open University. In Eds Mason, Robin & Kaye, Anthony, *Mindweave*, Pergamon Press, Oxford.

Mason, Robin (1994). *Using Communications Media in Open and Flexible Learning.* Open and Distance Learning Series. Kogan Page.

Mason, Robin (1996). STILE at the Open University: Summative evaluation. Internal CITE Report, Paper No. 221.

Murphy, Daniel (1994). Computer Mediated Communication (CMC) and the communication of technical Information in Aerospace. 32nd Aerospace Sciences Meeting and Exhibit January 10-13, 1994 / Reno, NV. *American Institute of Aeronautics and Aeronautics Inc, Report No AIAA- 94/0840.*

Newman, R. and Newman, J. (1993). Social Writing: Premises and Practices in Computerised Contexts. In Sharples eds *Computer Supported Cooperative Work.* Springer-Verlag.

Wegerif, Rupert (1995) Collaborative learning on TLO 94: creating an on-line community. *Open University CITE report No 212.*

Wilson, Tina & Whitelock, Denise (1996). Piloting a new approach; Making use of new technology to present a distance learning computer science course. *Association for Learning Technology Journal* (ALT-J), Volume 4, Number 1, pages 58 - 68.

Wilson, Tina & Whitelock, Denise (1997a). Facilitation of on-line learning environments: what works when teaching distance learning computer science students. Presented at the 2nd International Symposium, on Networked Learner Support, Sheffield, England, June 23rd-24th, 1997.

Wilson, Tina & Whitelock, Denise (1997b). Facilitating electronic communication; Evaluating computer science tutors' and students' interaction using computer mediated communication at a distance learning University. In, eds Richard Cornell and Kathy Ingram *An International Survey of Distance Education and Learning: From Smoke Signals to Satellite III*. A Report for the International Council for Educational Media (ICEM) pp. 74-94. Presented at the ICEM Media Week in Berlin Germany, March 1997.

Wilson, Tina & Whitelock, Denise (1997c). Hijacking Hypermedia and other Highways to learn computer science on a distance learning course. *Association for Learning Technology Journal* (ALT-J), Volume 5 number 2.

Wilson, Tina & Whitelock, Denise (1998a). What are the perceived benefits of participating in a CMC for distance learning computer science students. *Journal of Computers and Education,* Vol 30, No 3/4 pp. 259-269.

Wilson, Tina & Whitelock, Denise (1998b). Monitoring the on-line behaviour of distance learning students. *Journal of Computer Assisted Learning JCAL*, Vol. 14 pp 91 - 99.

Wilson, Tina & Whitelock, Denise (1998c). Is it worth it? Outside influences which affected participation in a CMC environment created for distance learning computer science students. *Internal Open University CALRG report, paper no. 178.*

10 Computer-Mediated Communication in Distance Education

BARBARA CANNONE-SYRCOS AND GEORGE SYRCOS
TEI PIRAEUS, GREECE

Abstract

In recent years emerging technologies for information exchange have put an increased pressure on universities and educators to provide alternative instructional delivery systems. Through the use of computers and telecommunications, computer-mediated communication (CMC) has emerged as an alternative mode of educational delivery. In particular, computer conferencing has become a powerful tool for instructional communication without the constraints of pre-determined meeting times or geographic locations. Unlike the format of pen-and-paper correspondence courses, CMC formats for distance education allow for learning environments that are more integrated and interactive. Today, CMC is one of the fastest growing technologies in terms of the number of educators and students using it for distance education purposes. In order for CMC to be successful, however, its integration into a curriculum requires the consideration of many parameters. This chapter will examine some of the more important course design issues as well as address special concerns and strengths of CMC-based instruction. Considering and resolving important design issues, however, is only part of the equation for a successful CMC-based program. Basic teaching practices cannot be left out. A few basic principles can help instructors in CMC-based programs and the issue of collaborative learning will also be discussed. Lastly, this chapter touches on some of the potential impacts on both students and faculty of an Asynchronous Learning Network (ALN) system.

Introduction

Fundamental to Computer Mediated Communication in education is that the capabilities of the computer are successfully utilised to facilitate the learning process between a group of instructors and students in an electronic virtual environment that is meant to partially or completely replace the environment of the physical classroom (Turoff, 1995). A large number of colleges currently offer remote courses using a number of forms of CMC. The flexibility and sophistication of software structures for supporting distance education vary from simple electronic mail systems or posting material on the World Wide Web to computer conferencing systems enhanced with advanced features designed specifically to support Learning Networks in which educators and learners are connected to each other as well as to the vast resources of the Internet. One such advanced conferencing system is the Asynchronous Learning Network (ALN) system called the Virtual Classroom [TM] being used at the New Jersey Institute of Technology (NJIT) for a little more than a decade. The Virtual Classroom [TM] is NJIT's trademarked name for versions of its Electronic Information Exchange System (EIES2) with special software enhancements that provide features that allow access to advanced educational experiences for distance students. Some of these features will be touched on later in this chapter. For now, factors to be considered when integrating CMC into a course or curriculum will be discussed.

CMC Implementation Consideration Factors

Course goals

The first factor to consider is course goals. As part of the course planning was, unless the goals of the course are clearly understood and educators understand how the technology will help fulfil these goals, it is senseless to integrate CMC. If CMC is to be integrated, then the issue arises as to how to do so and to what extent.

Integration

CMC is often used in conjunction with other traditional modes of educational communication for distance education. For example, NJIT offers two complete undergraduate degree programs via a mix of video plus Virtual Classroom (B.S. in Computer Science and the B.A. in Information Systems). For the courses in these programs, there can be many different successful media mix configurations. Possible configurations could include CMC plus one or two face-to-face meetings, or CMC with the use of distributed material, textbooks or course notes. A multimedia configuration could include CMC plus video or CMC plus audio or audiographic material, CD-ROM or other special PC based software. NJIT offers this type of multimedia arrangement where lecture type material is delivered via a mode that has both video and audio channels while the class discussions and student projects take place in a (mostly) text-oriented computer conferencing environment (Hiltz, 1997).

Just how CMC will be used in course curricula takes careful planning. As Bates (Bates, 1997) points out from his experience as one of the initial course team members that designed DT200 (An Introduction to Information Technology: Social and Technical Issues) at the UK Open University, CMC should not simply be added to all existing technology courses thus creating a tremendous workload for both course programmers and students, but rather deserves closer consideration. This point leads us to another important factor when considering using CMC in a distance education program, i.e. instructor and student readiness.

Readiness

It is not expected that most educators will master the current collection of protocols and software associated with CMC systems. However, an instructor's (author's) ability to use various tools to design course material and use CMC applications that will meet course and delivery goals is an important factor to consider. This factor will only become more important as CMC-based distance education programs begin to utilize the power of multimedia technology. NJIT is currently developing such computer aided interactive multimedia courseware with a focus on manufacturing engineering (Turoff, 1995). Use of this "courseware" will demand an even greater readiness on the part of the course instructor.

In terms of student readiness, regardless of the mode of electronic communication, computer-mediated teaching in distance education requires that the student know or at least be familiar with this medium. This is, of course, not always the case, and without proper course design and Concise guidelines as to the usage of the CMC-based course sections, students may feel overly challenged and become discouraged. An example of preparing students can be seen with the Educational Technology Leadership (ETL) Masters degree program at George Washington University (GWU). No formal training in computer conferencing is given. However, students are provided with a handbook describing the Bulletin Board System (BBS) being used and also given a demonstration in the first class of every course televised. Studies show that the learning curve with regard to learning the operation of computer systems and telecommunications operations can be steep and thus so can be the cost of using CMC in distance education.

Costs

In colleges and schools today the cost of purchasing and supporting systems or accessing other networks is a significant "overhead" cost [Berge, Collins, 1995]. Added to this are the costs and inconvenience of hardware upgrades, repairs and replacements. There is also the consideration of reliability. Computer systems are not 100% reliable and problems causing inconvenience and wasted time will inevitably occur. Although there are special concerns and limitations to using CMC as a mode of educational delivery, there are also many benefits.

Benefits of CMC

The greatest and the most obvious benefit of CMC is its ability to liberate educational instruction from the constraints of distance and time. This asynchronous or "anytime/anywhere" nature of CMC-based programs allow many students and instructors to better coordinate their lives in terms of job, travel and family responsibilities. In the case of the Virtual Classroom [TM] at NJIT, participants may connect at any time from any location in the world accessible by the Internet or a reliable telephone system - there is no need to be online at the same time. Special software structures of its EIES2 store entries in a permanent, ordered transcript keeping the equivalent of "bookmarks" separating items that have already been seen from "new" items for each individual. CMC distance courses allow many people to fit the demands of a college degree program into their busy lives.

The ETL program at GWU, while using a BBS versus the Internet, also reports many benefits of computer conferencing in their master's program. In CMC-based programs, the fact that it is asynchronous means that students have more time for reflective thinking before having to answer problems or discuss issues. This can be especially beneficial to students who do not have good communication skills (not very verbal) and those who do not have a very good command of spoken English, as is probably the case for some proportion of foreign students. Those students thus have more time to formulate and present their thoughts than they would have had in the conventional classroom. Studies have repeatedly shown that another positive aspect of CMC is the high degree of interactivity. Interactivity is not only increased between student and instructor, but also increased amongst fellow classmates regardless of geographical location. This kind of online environment encourages an atmosphere of collaborative learning.

Collaborative Learning and Interactivity

Collaborative learning is defined as a learning process that emphasizes cooperative or group efforts among students and faculty. CMC-based courses provide an ideal environment for collaborative learning. Online classes give students the opportunity to see the work of others and compare their ideas with those of their classmates versus the traditional classroom (TC), where a student's work is seen by only the instructor. Because online environments allow for students to see the work of others, they learn not only from their own work but also from the work of classmates. An example of this is in the case of assignments in the ETL program that are meant for the basis of discussions where student responses are posted as public messages so everyone can "see" each others work. On the other hand, feedback from the instructor to the student is normally sent as a private message so that comments can be candid, if need be. Online classrooms, by their very nature, encourage group interaction and collaborative learning. The ETL program at GWU often has the students do assignments as teams, each team member receiving the same grade. The effectiveness and impact study at GWU (Kearsley, Lynch, Wizer, 1998) has found that students learn that by drawing on the strengths of the group to produce a better solution proves much more effective than individual and competitive efforts. While the platform for collaborative learning is there, in cases where group projects are not part of the course structure, it is not a given that the process will occur.

Hiltz (1997) points out that it is not enough to make an ALN available and then let students know that they can use it for questions and discussions concerning the readings at anytime they like. Many students in fact may never use it for this purpose at all. Instead, from years of experience with the VC at NJIT, Hiltz reports that it is important that from the very beginning of the course, that collaborative learning is established through substantial contributions by the students to class discussions. An exception holds for the first week of courses due to the fact that many distance students have problems obtaining all the books, videotapes and other materials by the first course week. Therefore in the first week the assignment should draw upon general knowledge, posted material or individual experiences. After this point, there are various strategies to apply collaborative learning.

An example of a collaborative learning strategy is NJIT's seminar-style presentations and discussions where the students become the teachers. Small groups or individuals must select and research a topic not assigned to the rest of the class. They then prepare a written summary of the most important points in the material to present to the class and also lead a class discussion on the material. Such activities, although often difficult to conduct in TC's, have been shown to work very well in the VC mode even with fairly large classes of undergraduates. In addition to group projects, other examples of collaborative learning strategies include debates, case study discussions, simulation and role-playing exercises, collaborative compositions of research plans, essays and stories, sharing of homework solutions and "ask an expert".

In the case of technical courses, it is often difficult to think how some of the most interesting collaborative learning structures can be applied. However, there is at least one type of collaborative assignment that has proved effective no matter how technical the course. A strategy that is practically guaranteed to engage students in thinking about the important material in the unit and interacting around this material is to have students make up one or two questions that test the understanding of a specific topic and would be suitable for an examination. As a homework assignment, in addition to making up their questions, the students are asked to answer at least one question suggested by another student. Grading of students on the quality and quantity of their questions and solutions has proved quite effective, especially in the case of American students who tend not to participate in optional activities but will do so if such efforts result in a better grade. The intense interactivity of collaborative learning also brings with it a barrage of personality and social psychological factors that deserve consideration.

Social & psychological factors

CMC is at present primarily text only with a consequential reduction in social cues. This aspect proves to be a filter for possible discrimination due to racial/cultural differences, physical handicaps or disabilities as well as simple personality factors. Students and instructors do not know what others look or sound like and all are viewed by the thoughts and ideas they present. This is not always the case in the TC. Some see this as a "protective ignorance" surrounding one's social roles, rank and status (Berge, Collins 1995). Perhaps as "coined" this expression will serve us when we think of the future of CMC-distance education. Graduating classes will in the not too distant future consist of a large international population where it will be beneficial to all, that in cases where nationality and religion are not the course topic, that all in the class are kept "ignorant" in this area. In this way, individuals will be judged on their course work performance excluding irrelevant social factors. Whether the lack of face-to-face interaction and social cues is an advantage of CMC in education is debatable among authors. Whereas some believe that CMC deceases the sense of isolation felt by participants, others believe that it increases it and may even lead to "computer addiction".

Teaching Strategies

Teaching strategies or techniques in the online classroom are different than those in the TC. In a computer conferencing context, it is very difficult to lecture, but rather instructors must lead discussions organize online activities/projects and provide assignment feedback as well as serve as a resource. Because of the interactive and collaborative nature of CMC, online courses are much more student-centred versus teacher controlled. Another significant differentiating factor is the heavy workload that an online course creates. Impact studies of the ETL program found instructors spending 1-2 hours per day per class online was not unusual. Multiply this by a normal workload of three courses and it is apparent that it is a substantial amount of time.

The ETL program has found it impossible for one instructor to handle the workload for more than 40 students so classes are divided into sections of 30-40 students (a sub-conference) with a teaching assistant assigned to each section. While the instructor is still responsible for answering questions directly from students concerning course content, managing grade appeals and supervising the assistants, it is the assistants who moderate discussions and grade most assignments. Just as there is no single formula for successful teaching in the TC, there are a variety of techniques that can be successful in the CMC environment. From more than a decade of experience with the Virtual Classroom [TM] at NJIT, Hiltz (1995) reports there are, however, four basic principles one should keep in mind for successful teaching in the VC. The four basic principles proposed are of media richness, instructor responsiveness, organisation and interaction.

Media Richness

In CMC courses, lectures do not include things found in the TC such as an occasional joke, gestures or pleasant personal characteristics, but rather there is only the screen and/or printed matter. To maintain interest, the instructor should use the written language skilfully with an injection of humour or metaphor. It is suggested that instead of trying to deliver an entire lecture in written format online, that instead it is given in small segments with opportunities for participation. For purely lecture type material, printed or pre-recorded material is best.

Responsiveness

Another basic and important principal to keep in mind is that of responsiveness. It is one thing in the TC where students receive an immediate response to their questions and another case with online classrooms. It can be very frustrating for a student to be stuck in the middle of a difficult assignment and have to wait for a response. The flip side to this, however, is that students in online classrooms may ask questions, participate in ongoing discussions and receive feedback on a daily basis whereas TC students have only a few hours per week for their questions. The time an instructor spends responding to questions online each day varies, but it can become quite substantial. Thus, with online classes, the role of the instructor changes somewhat, from a few hours a week (TC) to being a "perpetual professor" where the teaching is continuous (VC). The third and quite important principal to keep in mind is that of organisation.

Organisation

Organisation is a critical component to success due to the large amount of information that will be transferred. With a typical class size of 20-30 students each entering a minimum of two comments per week plus the material entered by the instructor, a typical course will have at least 100 new entries per week. Unless well organized, things could become quite chaotic. It is important that the instructor establish a schedule, dividing the course into modules of fixed time duration of say 1, 1.5 or 2 weeks. In this way students can plan when they will need to get online and when assignments will be due. This structure allows the entire class to move through the course material in an orderly fashion.

An example used by Hiltz (1997) at NJIT for one course is to post online "electures" every Tuesday and assignments on Thursday. These assignments are due in nine days. With this schedule, students will in general sign on at least 3 times per week; one time for the electure and to respond to it, once to get the new assignment and once to upload their completed assignments. In order for class interaction to be meaningful, it is important that the class move through the modules together. For this reason, although online courses may be self-paced on an individual basis within a period of time, the over-all course schedule must be adhered to. When posting assignments, due dates must be firmly set and penalties for lateness enforced. This will prevent students from falling behind and potentially confusing class discussion by talking about assignments weeks after their due dates.

Interaction

Two further principles, interactivity and collaboration, probably play the greatest roles in terms of how students compare traditional modes of educational delivery with that of the online course. The amount and quality of interaction between students and instructors and among students themselves is very important. Although not always easy to achieve, if the instructor can get students into this collaborative approach to learning, they will work together in ways that arc rarely scan in the TC. Hiltz believes that here lies both the key and the challenge for successful teaching in online courses. As discussed earlier, online courses are ideal environments for collaborative learning not only among students and instructors, but also among a class and wider academic and non-academic communities as well. Online classes being relatively new, their results of impact studies may not be all encompassing, however some results are presented in the next section.

Impacts

Preliminary findings al NJIT on the impacts on students and potential impacts on faculty suggest the following (Hiltz, 1997). The overall ratings of courses by students who have completed ALN based courses at NJIT are equal to or superior to those for traditional courses. Whereas the number of non-completions and dropouts was somewhat higher for students in the ALN based courses, the grade distributions for those who did complete the courses, tended to be similar to those for traditional courses.

Also discovered was that at the beginning of courses, both students and faculty needed more start-up time in order to solve the "logistics" associated with ALN delivery. After a decade of experience with ALN delivery, Hiltz has observed that although the specific nature of technical and logistical problems change over time, they are however persistent. Below is a review of some of the results found al NJIT (Hiltz 1997).

For sections using the VC, the post-course questionnaire administered instructed students to compare their experiences in traditional face-to-face college courses with their experiences in the course they had just completed. The results found that 71% felt that ALNs provided better access to their professor (it is dependent, however, on the instructor being available online at least once a day). Also despite reported problems of some such as busy lines, 69% still felt that the VC was, overall, "more convenient".

In terms of interactivity and collaborative learning, only 15% did not feel they took a more active part in the course. The results also showed that "collaborative learning" with it's intentional motivational and learning consequences did take place. Only 9% disagreed that reading the assignments of other students was useful, whereas 55% felt more motivated to work hard on their assignments for this reason. An interim result also related to interaction and motivation showed that 13% felt that they did not have to work as hard for the online class whereas 67% disagreed.

An overall indicator of student satisfaction is whether or not students would choose to take another ALN course. Only 20% agreed with a statement saying they would not do so, whereas 58% indicated that they would. Asked if they had learned more than they would have in a TC, students were not as sure; but 40% felt they had whereas 21% felt they had not. Students were also not so sure as to whether or not the VC increased the efficiency of educational delivery; but 47% felt it does compared to 23% who felt it does not. Students were more sure, however, on whether or not VC "increased the quality of education"; 58% saying it did, while only 20% saying it did not. This same study at NJIT also reported some preliminary impressions on faculty impacts as gathered from online "faculty lounge" discussions as well as completed course reports.

The impact on faculty workload is the first and foremost consideration. The workload is especially great the first time a faculty member prepares a course. There is the preparation of ALN online materials, moderating class conferences and daily interactions with students through email in addition to preparing the weekly modules. Once VC delivery material is developed, the instructor has gained experience and the class size is kept at a level of 25 or less, the amount of work has shown to be about the same as that in the TC. However, it should be stressed that class size is a critical factor to keep in mind. The amount of work the course facilitator will have is directly proportional to the number of students. Also noted at NJIT was the difficulty some instructors found in "rounding" up students for a discussion. Instructors feeling first like system administrators for conferencing and head-hunters and only then lecturers.

Impact issues also exist that need consideration by policy-making bodies of universities. One such issue is that of the impacts of ALNs on the content and size of the faculty teaching loads. It seems only logical to have a policy established for class sizes of more than 30 students, such as that at GWU. When class sizes exceed 30-40 students, teaching assistants are assigned or classes are divided into sub-groups. Also are the ongoing issues of intellectual property (who owns the rights to ALN material created by professors), compensation for work in course material preparation for distance delivery and also support to faculty to learn the new techniques and skills needed to succeed in an ALN environment.

Thoughts for the Future

Computer-mediated communication in distance education is a rapidly growing technology and seems to be the way many courses will be offered in the 21st Century. Its future, however, is dependent on overcoming some of the difficulties presented in this chapter such as providing faculty training and dealing with initial increased faculty workloads. There must also be adequate motivation or compensation given to faculty members if they are to take time away from their research to devote towards preparing course material in electronic form. An example of such motivation could come in the form of reduced teaching workloads. This is an area where much further consideration is needed in order to determine which tasks may be offloaded from the professor and assigned to assistants without jeopardizing quality.

At present most CMC-based distance education programs work with a combination of CMC (via Internet, conferencing systems, bulletin boards, etc.) plus video or broadcasts and distributed material (books, notes, etc.). In the future, however, most students will probably have multi-media work stations where CD-ROM based or World Wide Web-based digitised video modules replace broadcasts and videos. In the long run, ALNs will probably lead to a decrease in the number of colleges and universities, as larger institutions develop distance-education programs that students anywhere can enrol in and thus will choose over "second rate" local colleges [Hiltz 1997]. In general, ALNs will contribute to a change in the role universities and colleges play, shifting from institutions geared towards the 18 to 22 year age group, to being educational institutions with a variety of degree programs designed to meet the needs of students of all ages.

References

Bates, A.W. (1995) Technology, Open Learning and Distance Education, *Routledge Studies in Distance Education*, London, NY and Canada, (1995, reprint 1997).

Berge, Z. and Collins, M. (1995) Computer-Mediated Communication and the Online Classroom in *Distance Learning, Computer-Mediated Communication Magazine*, 2(4), p. 6.

Berge, Z. and Collins, M. (1995) Computer-Mediated Communication and the Online Classroom in *Higher Education, Computer-Mediated Communication Magazine*, 2(3), p. 39.

Hiltz, S. R. (1997) Impacts of college-level courses via Asynchronous Learning Nctworks: Some Preliminary Results, for *The Journal of Asynchronous Learning Networks*.

Hiltz, S.R. (1995) Teaching in a Virtual Classroom [TM], 1995 *International Conference on Computer Assisted Instruction ICCAI 95*, March 7-10, Hsinchu, Taiwan.

Kearsley, G., Lynch,W., Wizer, D. (1995) The Effectiveness and Impact of Computer Conferencing in Graduate Education, (posted on WWW 5/8/95)- based on an article published in Educational Technology Magazine.

Moore, M.G. (1993) is Teaching Like Flying? A Total Systems View of Distance Education, American *Journal of Distance Education*, 7(1), 1-10.

Turoff, M. (1995) Designing a Virtual Classroom [TM], 1995 *International Conference on Computer Assisted Instruction ICCAI 95*, March 7-10, Hsinchu, Taiwan.

Wells, R. (1992) Computer-mediated Communication for Distance Education: An International Review of Design, Teaching and Institutional Issues, University Park, PA: American Center for the Study of Distance Education, Pennsylvania State University.